# Study Guide

to accompany

# A Child's World
## Infancy Through Adolescence
### Ninth Edition

Diane E. Papalia

Sally Wendkos Olds

Ruth Duskin Feldman

Prepared by
Wendy Micham
*Victor Valley College*

Mc
Graw
Hill

Boston   Burr Ridge, IL   Dubuque, IA   Madison, WI   New York   San Francisco   St. Louis
Bangkok   Bogotá   Caracas   Kuala Lumpur   Lisbon   London   Madrid   Mexico City
Milan   Montreal   New Delhi   Santiago   Seoul   Singapore   Sydney   Taipei   Toronto

## McGraw-Hill Higher Education

*A Division of The McGraw-Hill Companies*

Study Guide to accompany
A CHILD'S WORLD: INFANCY THROUGH ADOLESCENCE, NINTH EDITION
PAPALIA/OLDS/FELDMAN

Published by McGraw-Hill Higher Education, an imprint of The McGraw-Hill Companies, Inc.,
1221 Avenue of the Americas, New York, NY 10020. Copyright © The McGraw-Hill Companies,
Inc., 2002, 1999, 1996. All rights reserved.

This book is printed on acid-free paper.

1 2 3 4 5 6 7 8 9 0 QPD QPD 0 3 2 1

ISBN 0-07-241417-0

www.mhhe.com

# Table of Contents

## Preface

## Part One: Entering A Child's World

## Part Two: Beginnings

## Part Three: Infancy and Toddlerhood

## Part Four: Early Childhood

## Part Five: Middle Childhood

## Part Six: Adolescence

# Preface
## <u>To The Student</u>

This Study Guide with Readings has been designed to help you get the most out of *A Child's World*, Ninth Edition, by Diane E. Papalia, Sally Wendkos Olds, and Ruth Duskin Feldman. It is not intended as a substitute for *A Child's World*; rather, it is just what its title implies - a guide to help you absorb and interpret the material in the text. Although some of the material in your textbook will be familiar to you (since you once inhabited the world of childhood), much of it will be new; and you must now see all of it from a new perspective, as an adult and a student of child development. Using this Study Guide will increase your understanding of the material and improve your ability to remember it, to apply it, and to build on it throughout this course, in related courses, and in your own life.

The Study Guide will help you to:

- o Organize and focus your learning
- o Check your mastery of the material in the text
- o Practice dealing with typical examination formats
- o Think analytically about the subject matter
- o Broaden your perspective on child development

# How This Study Guide Is Organized

The Study Guide's seventeen chapters correspond to Chapters 1 to 17 of *A Child's World*. Each chapter of the Study Guide begins with a brief Overview of the text chapter, reiterated the Guideposts for Study [as mentioned in the text chapter], and has the following parts:

1.  Chapter Review
2.  Chapter Quiz
3.  Answer Key

Let's take a look at each of these, to give you an understanding of how the Study Guide works and how you'll be using it.

CHAPTER REVIEW

The Chapter Review is a way to organize and focus your learning. It will help you identify and reexamine important material in the text chapter and also help you decide which material will need further study.

The Review is divided into sections that correspond to the major headings in the text chapter. This format lets you break your study into manageable "chunks" and makes it easier for you to locate information in the text, check answers, and concentrate on areas where you need to do more work.

Typically, each section of the Review has three elements: Framework, Important Terms, and Learning Objectives.

Framework:  The Framework is an outline of all the subheadings in the text section. (When there are no subheadings within a section, this element is omitted.) The Framework shows you the section at a glance and indicates the relationship among different topics taken up in the section. You might think of it as a road map. You can use it to preview the section; you should refer to it frequently as you read, to get your bearings; and later, you can use it to remind yourself where you have been.

You can also use the Framework to guide your reading by using the "questioning" approach. You'll notice that some of the text headings are in the form of questions; others can be rephrased as questions, which you can keep in mind as you read. For example, in Chapter 1, you'll find the heading, "Influences on Children's Development." You might ask yourself, "What are the influences on children's development? When do these influences occur?" If you can give a tentative answer, jot it down. Then, when you find the answer in the text, check to see if you were on the right track.

Important Terms:  Important Terms is a fill-in-the-blanks exercise, which covers all the "key terms" in the text section. It checks your knowledge of terms and meanings; it gives you practice with completion-type test items; and, when you have filled it in, it will serve as a glossary for the section, to be used for reference and review. (For text sections without key terms, the Important Terms exercise is omitted.)

Can you fill in the blanks without referring to the text? If you do need to consult the text, can you go directly to the passage you need? If you must turn to the text often, or if you have trouble finding the information you want, you'll know that you need additional study.

Check your work against the Answer Key. Your wrong answers will let you know where more work is needed.

Learning Objectives: The Learning Objectives are a list of tasks you should be able to accomplish when you have studied the section. To check your understanding of the text material, see if you can accomplish each objective without recourse to the text. If you need to look at the text, note how readily you can locate the necessary information.

You can use the space provided below each objective to make brief notes. But the Learning Objectives can also serve another purpose, since they resemble essay-type test items. Writing out complete, formal answers to some or all of them - on separate paper - will give you needed practice in the essay format.

## CHAPTER QUIZ

The Chapter Quiz will check your mastery of the text material. It also gives you practice with three types of questions often found on tests:
1.  Matching
2.  Multiple choice
3.  True-or-false

Take the quiz when you are reasonably confident about your mastery of the entire chapter. This is a closed-book test. Put the textbook away - far away, if you are easily tempted - and allow about as much time to take the quiz as you would have for a classroom examination.

As you take the quiz, pay attention to your "comfort level." Are you uncertain or uneasy about many items? Do you find that you must skip many items? Do you find that you are often just guessing? If so, stop and review the text again.

If your comfort level is high - that is, if you're confident about most of the questions - complete the quiz and then check the Answer Key. You should not be satisfied unless you've gotten almost all the answers right. Remember that this quiz is easier than an actual classroom examination because you take it when you decide you're ready, you are not under so much tension, and you can pace yourself. If you miss more than a few (very few) questions, restudy the material.

## ANSWER KEY

The Answer Key for each chapter gives answers, for the Important Terms exercise and for the entire Chapter Quiz.

Use the Answer Key wisely, to check your work. Don't use it as a crutch; don't "peek" when you should be testing your recall. If you misuse the answers, you'll be cheating no one but yourself.

# Before You Begin: Learning Aids In Your Textbook

The Ninth Edition of *A Child's World* itself contains several important study aids. You should take advantage of these features as you read the text.

Chapter Contents: On the opening page of each chapter you'll see a listing of major headings. Take a few minutes to examine it, asking yourself, "What topics does this chapter cover, and how are they organized?"

Focus Vignettes: Each chapter of the text begins with a Focus vignette: a true story from the childhood of a well-known person. Reading and thinking about the vignette will prepare you for some of the important concepts and issues to be discussed in the chapter. As you read the chapter, think back to the Focus vignette and ask yourself how it relates to the material you are learning.

Guideposts for Study: Following the Focus vignette, you will find some questions designed to direct your attention to significant material covered in the chapter. These integrate the Preview questions that appeared in the eighth edition of *A Child's World*. A good way to make use of this learning aid is to check off each Guidepost for Study as you find the answer in the text, making a brief note of the answer and the page or pages where it appears. When you've finished the chapter, turn back to the Guidepost for Study. Can you answer each one fully without referring to the text?

Checkpoints: In the margins, following major sections of each chapter, you will find Checkpoints designed to help you check your knowledge of what you have read. Many of the Checkpoints are similar to (but generally broader than) the Learning Objectives in this Study Guide, and you can use them in the same way, answering the questions or doing the tasks either mentally or in writing. Be sure that you can "pass" each Checkpoint before going on to the next section of text; if you cannot do so, you need to review the section you have just read.

Key Terms: In each chapter, the authors identify certain "key terms." These are printed in bold italic in the running text, defined in the margins, and then listed at the end of the chapter in the summary (with page references). Whenever you encounter a key term, stop and read its definition. Is the definition clear to you? (If not, reread the explanation in the text.) Can you think of a specific example? When you've finished a chapter, use the list at the end to review the vocabulary and check your mastery of it.

Boxes: The boxes illuminate many topics covered in the text. Read them as carefully as the text itself and ask yourself questions about them: "How does this box relate to the subject matter in the text?" "Why was this topic chosen for highlighting?" If a box takes up a controversial issue, what is your opinion?

Tables and Illustrations: Pay close attention to tables, figures, and photographs. They illustrate, summarize, or crystallize material in the text, making it easier to understand and remember.

Consider This: These thought-provoking questions following each chapter of the text are meant to stimulate your thinking and to help you see the relevance of theory and research to real life situations, problems, and issues. You may wish to write out answers, as suggested above, to give you practice in answering essay-type questions.

Summary: The summary at the end of each chapter is organized under each of the major chapter headings and includes all of the key terms in boldface. It gives a quick review of the main points that were covered in the chapter and is another good way for you to check your learning. Is each of the items familiar to you? Can you expand on each?

Glossary: The glossary at the end of the book brings together all the key terms from every chapter, in alphabetical order, with their definitions and with page references to the text. It is useful for reference and review.

Bibliography: You may not have thought of the bibliography as a study aid, but it can be: it is an excellent guide to books and articles for further research.

People who teach and write about study skills will tell you that a crucial part of learning effectively is being an "active reader" - being alert, perceptive, and involved as you read. You'll find that using these special features in *A Child's World* will help you become an active reader and thus a more efficient learner.


Acknowledgments

I would like to thank the author team of *A Child's World* for continuing to write such a wonderful accessible text; and Ruth Duskin Feldman for her terrific work on the eighth edition of this Study Guide. She gave me such a solid basis from which to update this edition. I would also like to especially thank the editorial team at McGraw-Hill, and my family for their continued support and encouragement throughout this project.

*Wendy Micham*
*Victor Valley College*

## OVERVIEW

Chapter 1 introduces you to the study of child development. In this chapter, the authors:

❑ Define child development and explain how it has evolved

❑ Discuss the emerging consensus of fundamental points in child development

❑ Outline the aspects of development to be studied for each period of childhood

❑ Point out several types of influences on how children develop and the contextual levels within which influences occur

## GUIDEPOSTS FOR STUDY

1.1 What is child development and how has its study evolved?

1.2 What are six fundamental points on which consensus has emerged in the study of child development?

1.3 What do developmental scientists study?

1.4 What are the three major aspects and five periods of child development?

## CHAPTER 1 REVIEW

### Section I  The Study of Child Development: Then and Now
FRAMEWORK FOR SECTION I

A.    Early Approaches

B.    Studying the Life Span

C.    New Frontiers

D.    An Emerging Consensus

## IMPORTANT TERMS FOR SECTION I

**Completion:** Fill in the blanks to complete the definitions of key terms for this section of Chapter 1.

1. **Child development:** Scientific study of change and _____ from conception through adolescence.

2. In the studying of child development, scientists argue about the relative importance of _____ and _____ .

3. Today the study of child development is part of the broader study of _____ which covers the entire life span.

4. The study of development is increasingly directed to the_____ ,_____,_____, and social policies applied to children.

5. The exploration of child development has evolved and matured to where today, there is a broad _____ regarding _____fundamental points that have emerged.

# LEARNING OBJECTIVES FOR SECTION I

After reading and reviewing this section of Chapter 1, you should be able to do the following: (Note: Here and throughout this study guide, when you are asked to give examples, try to think of examples other than those given in the text.)

1.  Distinguish the difference between "nature" and "nurture". Give examples of how each influences development.

2.  Summarize the six fundamental points of agreement that have emerged from the study of child development.

3.  Tell how the early parental and children's diaries and baby biographies contributed to the evolution of the study of child development.

4.  List and describe four trends that led to the scientific study of child development.

5. Tell how the study of child development fits into the study of human development.

6. Summarize the contributions of ten pioneers in the study of child development.

## Section II  The Study of Child Development : Basic Concepts

### FRAMEWORK FOR SECTION II

A.  Developmental Processes: Change and Stability

B.  Domains of Development

C.  Periods of Development

### IMPORTANT TERMS FOR SECTION II

**Completion:** Fill in the blanks to complete the definitions of key terms for this section of Chapter 1.

1. _____ change: Change in number or amount, such as in height, weight, or size of vocabulary.

2. _____ change: Change in kind, structure, or organization, such as the change from nonverbal to verbal communication.

3. Growth of the body and brain, sensory capacities, motor skills, and health are part of the _____ development.

4. Cognitive development includes mental abilities such as _____,_____,_____,_____, and moral reasoning.

3

5. Change and stability in personality, emotional life, and social relationships constitute _____ development.

6. An idea about how people view members of their particular society on the basis of shared subjective perceptions or assumptions defines _____ _____ .

## LEARNING OBJECTIVES FOR SECTION II

After reading and reviewing this section of Chapter 1, you should be able to do the following: (Note: Here and throughout this study guide, when you are asked to give examples, try to think of examples other than those given in the text.)

1. Explain the difference between qualitative and quantitative change and give at least one example of each.

2. Name the main aspects (domains) of development and give an example of how each interacts with one of the other two.

3. List the five periods into which your text divides childhood and identify the approximate age range and at least three major developments of each period.

## Section III  Influences on Development

### FRAMEWORK FOR SECTION III

A.    Heredity, Environment, and Maturation

B.    Major Contextual Influences

    1.  Family

    2.  Socioeconomic Status and Neighborhood

    3.  Culture and Ethnicity

    4.  The Historical Context

C.    Normative and Nonnormative Influences

D.    Timing of Influences: Critical or Sensitive Periods


### IMPORTANT TERMS FOR SECTION III

1.  _____: are differences among children in characteristic influences or development outcomes.

2.  _____: Inborn influences on development, carried on the genes inherited from the parents.

3.  **environment:** Totality of _____ influences on development, external to the self.

4.  _____ :Unfolding of a genetically-influenced, often age-related, _____ of physical changes and behavior patterns, including the readiness to master new abilities.

5.  **nuclear family:** Two-generational economic, kinship, and living unit made up of parents and their biological or _____ children.

6.  **extended family:** Multigenerational kinship network of parents, children, and more distant relatives, sometimes living  together in an _____ - _____ _____ .

7.  **socioeconomic status (SES):** Combination of economic and social factors, including income, _____, and occupation.

8.  _____: Group united by ancestry, race, religion, language, and/or national origins, which contribute to a sense of shared identity.

9.  _____: A society's or group's total way of life, including customs, traditions, beliefs, values, language, and physical products—all behavior passed on from adults to children.

10.  _____ characteristic of an event that occurs in a similar way for most people in a group.

11.  _____influences are unusual events that happen to a particular person, or an event that happens at an unusual time of life.

12.  _____ **period:** Specific time during development when a given event will have the greatest impact.

13.  **plasticity:** _____of performance.

14. _____ :Group of people who share a similar experience, such as growing up at the same time and in the same place.

## LEARNING OBJECTIVES FOR SECTION III

After reading and reviewing this section of Chapter 1, you should be able to do the following. (Note: Here and throughout this study guide, when you are asked to give examples, try to think of examples other than those given in the text.)

1. Distinguish between the influences of heredity, environment, and maturation.

2. Explain how socioeconomic status and risk factors can affect developmental outcomes.

3. Distinguish between ethnicity and culture, and explain how the ethnic composition of a society can influence cultural change.

4. Explain what it means for minority groups to acculturate.

5. Identify three types of experimental influences on children's development, and give an example of each

6. Explain the difference between critical periods and sensitive periods, and give at least one example of each.

## CHAPTER 1 QUIZ

**Multiple-Choice**: Circle the choice that best completes or answers each item.

1. The English naturalist who originated the theory of evolution, which held that all species developed through *natural selection* was
   a. G. Stanley Hall
   b. John Locke
   c. Charles Darwin
   d. Alfred Binet

2. Qualitative change involves change in
   a. amount
   b. kind
   c. both amount and kind
   d. either amount or kind, depending on the specific situation

3. The study of development can be viewed through the 'nature' side – or genetics, while the 'nurture' side refers to
   a. biology
   b. experience
   c. heredity
   d. none of the above

4. The prenatal stage is defined as lasting until
   a. the pregnant woman "feels life"
   b. the fetus's basic body structures and organs are formed
   c. the fetus's brain develops
   d. birth

5. Culture appears to exert a strong influence on
   a. the age at which babies learn to walk
   b. the sequence of learning to talk
   c. sentence structure
   d. none of the above

6. Which of the following is an example of a normative history-graded influence?
   a. puberty
   b. a disabling accident
   c. the end of the Cold War
   d. retirement

7. The unfolding of a natural sequence of physical and behavioral changes, including readiness to master new abilities refers to
   a. heredity
   b. environment
   c. acculturation
   d. maturation

8. An early, influential baby biography was written by
   a. Charles Darwin
   b. Lewis Terman
   c. John Locke
   d. Jean Jacques Rousseau

**True or False?** In the blank following each item, write T (for true) or F (for false). In the space below each item, if the statement is false, rewrite it to make it true

1. A child's growth in height is an example of qualitative change. _____

2. Acculturation means the same as assimilation. _____

3. Early childhood is the years from 6 to 11._____

4. Cross-cultural research is valuable because the impact of certain influences on children varies in different societies. _____

5. *Critical period* means a specific time when a given event or its absence has the greatest impact on development. _____

6. Today, developmentalists may view the capacity for language acquisition to be more resilient than once believed._____

# ANSWER KEY FOR CHAPTER 1

**CHAPTER 1 REVIEW**

**Important Terms for Section I**
1. continuity
2. nature and nurture
3. human development
4. rearing, education, health
5. consensus, six

**Important Terms for Section II**
1. quantitative
2. qualitative
3. physical
4. learning, memory, language, thinking
5. psychosocial
6. social construction

**Important Terms for Section III**
1. Individual differences
2. Heredity
3. nonhereditary
4. Maturation, sequences
5. adopted
6. extended-family household
7. education
8. ethnic group
9. Culture
10. Normative
11. Nonnormative
12. Critical
13. Modifiability
14. Cohort

**CHAPTER 1 QUIZ**

**Multiple-Choice**
1. c
2. b
3. b
4. d
5. a
6. c
7. d
8. a

**True or False**
1. F-growth in amount is quantitative
2. F-Acculturation is not adopting, but, instead, adapting in some ways
3. F- Early Childhood is the years from 3 to 6
4. T
5. T
6. T

# CHAPTER 2
# A CHILD'S WORLD: HOW WE DISCOVER IT

## OVERVIEW

Chapter 2 describes the various ways in which child development is theorized and studied. In this chapter the authors:

❑ Discuss which has more impact on development: heredity or environment
❑ Discuss several important issues and perspectives from which child development has been viewed
❑ Describe the major types of methods for studying child development and discuss advantages and disadvantages of each
❑ Discuss ethical issues regarding research on children

## GUIDEPOSTS FOR STUDY

2.1   What purposes do theories serve?

2.2   What are three basic theoretical issues on which developmental scientists differ?

2.3   What are five theoretical perspectives on child development, and what are some theories representative of each?

2.4   How do developmental scientists study children, and what are some advantages and disadvantages of each research method?

2.5   What ethical problems may arise in research on children?

## CHAPTER 2 REVIEW

**Section I  Basic Theoretical Issues**

### FRAMEWORK FOR SECTION I

A.      Issue 1: Which is More Important – Heredity or Environment?

B.      Issue 2: Are Children Active or Passive in Their Development?

C.      Issue 3: Is Development Continuous, or Does It Occur in Stages?

D.      An Emerging Consensus

### IMPORTANT TERMS FOR SECTION I

**Completion:** Fill in the blanks to complete the definitions of key terms for this section of Chapter 2.

1. **theory:** Coherent set of related concepts that seeks to organize and _____/_____ data.
2. **hypotheses:** Possible _____ for phenomena, used to predict the outcome of research.
3. **mechanistic model:** Model, based on the machine as a metaphor, that views development as a passive, predictable response to internal and external _____ , focuses on quantitative development, and studies phenomena by  analyzing the operation of their component parts.
4. **organismic model:** Model that views development as internally initiated by an active person or organism, and as occurring in a universal sequence or qualitatively _____ stages of maturation.

### LEARNING OBJECTIVES FOR SECTION I

After reading and reviewing this section of Chapter 2, you should be able to do the following. (Remember: When you are asked to give examples, try to think of examples other than those given in the text.

1.Discuss three key issues in the study of child development, tell where two basic theoretical models stand on these issues, and summarize the emerging consensus on these issues.

**Section II Theoretical Perspectives**

FRAMEWORK FOR SECTION II

A.      Perspective 1: Psychoanalytic
   1.   Sigmund Freud: Psychosexual Development
   2.   Erik Erikson: Psychosocial Development
B.      Perspective 2: Learning
   1.   Learning Theory 1: Behaviorism
   2.   Learning Theory 2: Social Learning (Social Cognitive) Theory
C.      Perspective 3: Cognitive
   1.   Jean Piaget's Cognitive-Stage Theory
   2.   The Information-Processing Approach
   3.   Neo-Piagetian Theories
   4.   The Cognitive Neuroscience Approach
D.      Perspective 4: Ethological
E.      Perspective 5: Contextual
   1.   Urie Bronfenbrenner's Bioecological Theory
   2.   Lev Vygotsky's Sociocultural Theory
F.      How Theory and Research Work Together


IMPORTANT TERMS FOR SECTION II

**Completion: Fill in the blanks to complete the definitions of key terms for this section of Chapter 2.**

1. _____ **perspective:** View of development concerned with unconscious forces motivating behavior.
2. **psychosexual development:** In Freudian theory, an unvarying sequence of stages of personality development during infancy, childhood, and adolescence, regarding_____ of the genitals.
3. **id:** In Freudian theory, the instinctual aspect of personality (present at birth) that operates on the _____ principle, seeking immediate gratification.
4. **ego:** In Freudian theory, an aspect of personality that develops during infancy and operates on the _____ principle, seeking acceptable means of gratification in dealing with the real world.
5. **superego:** In Freudian theory, the aspect of personality that represents socially-approved values; it develops around the age of 5 or 6 as a result of _____ with the parent of the same sex.
6. **psychosocial development:** In _____'s theory, the socially and culturally influenced process of development of the ego, or self; it consists of eight maturationally determined stages throughout the life span, each revolving around a particular crisis or turning point in which the person is faced with achieving a healthy balance between alternative positive and negative traits.
7. **trust vs. mistrust:** The virtue of _____ develops during this stage of Erikson's developmental theory.
8. **learning perspective:** View of development concerned with changes in behavior that result from experience, or _____ to the environment; the two major branches are behaviorism and social-learning theory.
9. **learning:** Long-term change in behavior that occurs as a result of _____.
10. **behaviorism:** Learning theory that emphasizes the study of observable behaviors and events and the _____ role of environment in causing behavior.
11. **classical conditioning:** Kind of _____ in which a previously neutral stimulus (one that does not originally elicit a particular response) acquires the power to elicit the response after the stimulus is repeatedly associated with another stimulus that ordinarily does elicit the response.
12. **operant conditioning:** Kind of learning in which a person tends to repeat a behavior that has been _____ or to cease a behavior that has been punished.
13. **reinforcement:** In operant conditioning, a stimulus experienced following a behavior, which _____ the probability that the behavior will be repeated.

14. **punishment:** In operant conditioning, a stimulus experienced following a behavior, which _____ the probability that the behavior will be repeated.

15. social-learning theory: Theory, proposed by Bandura, that behaviors are learned by observing and imitating _____. Also called social-cognitive theory.

16. _____ **learning:** In social-learning theory, learning that occurs through watching the behavior of others.

17. _____ **perspective:** View of development concerned with thought processes and the behavior that reflects those processes.

18. **organization:** In Piaget's terminology, integration of knowledge into a _____ to make sense of the environment.

19. _____: In Piaget's terminology, basic cognitive structures consisting of organized patterns of behavior used in different kinds of situations.

20. **adaptation:** In Piaget's terminology, adjustment to new information about the environment through the _____ processes of assimilation and accommodation.

21. _____: In Piaget's terminology, incorporation of new information into an existing cognitive structure.

22. _____: In Piaget's terminology, changes in an existing cognitive structure to include new information.

23. _____: In Piaget's terminology, the tendency to strive for equilibrium (balance) among cognitive elements within the organism and between it and the outside world.

24. _____-processing approach: Approach to the study of cognitive development by observing and analyzing the mental processes involved in perceiving and handling _____.

25. **ethological perspective:** View of development that focuses on the biological and _____ bases of behavior.

26. **contextual perspective:** View of development that sees the individual as inseparable from the _____ context.

27. **sociocultural theory:** _____'s theory that analyzes how specific cultural practices, particularly social interaction with adults, affect children's development.

28. **zone of** _____ **development (abbreviated** _____**):** Vygotsky's term for the level at which children can almost perform a task on their own and, with appropriate teaching, can perform it.

29. Bronfenbrenner's term for a setting in which a child interacts with others on an everyday, face-to-face basis_____.

## LEARNING OBJECTIVES FOR SECTION II

After reading and reviewing this section of Chapter 2, you should be able to do the following. (Remember: When you are asked to give examples, try to think of examples other than those given in the text.)

1. Explain how theories help scientists achieve the four goals of the study of child development.

2. Identify five major perspectives on child development and their main distinguishing features.

3. Name the five stages of psychosexual development, according to Freud's theory, and identify the approximate age range and chief characteristics of each stage.

4. Tell what causes fixation, according to Freud's theory, and give an example of its effect.

5. Name and describe the three major components of personality according to Freud's theory.

6. Explain how Erikson's theory of psychosocial development modifies and expands upon Freud's psychosexual theory.

7. Explain what Erikson meant by a crisis in personality and his view of the implications of the way in which the crisis at each stage of development is resolved.

8. Name and briefly describe the eight crises in Erikson's theory.

9. Who was Ivan Pavlov and how did his research influence Behaviorism?

10. Name the two major theories that take the learning perspective, and explain the similarities and differences between them.

11. Name and describe the two types of conditioning and give at least one example of each.

12. Explain the difference between negative reinforcement and punishment.

13. Describe how shaping can be used in behavioral modification and give an example.

14. Name three factors that influence children's choice of models, according to social-learning theory.

15. Describe Piaget's clinical method.

16. Identify and explain three principles that underlie cognitive growth, according to Piaget.

17. List and briefly describe Piaget's four stages of cognitive development.

18. Identify the basic assumptions, goals, and methods of the information-processing approach.

19. Give and example of how neo-Piagetian psychologists combine elements of Piaget's theory with the information-processing approach.

20. Identify the basic assumptions, goals, and methods of the ethological perspective, and discuss how it has been applied to the study of attachment.

21. Identify five levels of environmental influences, that, according to Bronfenbrenner, provide the context for understanding development, and give an example of each.

22. Identify the basic assumptions and concerns of Vygotsky's sociocultural theory, and discuss its practical relevance to teaching and learning.

## Section III  Research Methods

FRAMEWORK FOR SECTION III

A.    Sampling
B.    Forms of Data Collection
    1.    Self-Reports: Diaries, Interviews, Questionnaires
    2.    Behavioral and Performance Measures
    3.    Naturalistic and Laboratory Observation
C.    Basic Research Designs
    1.    Case Studies

       2. Ethnographic Studies

       3. Correlational Studies

       4. Experiments

D.     Developmental Research Designs

       1. Longitudinal, Cross-Sectional, and Sequential Studies

       2. Microgentic Studies

E.     Ethics of Research

## IMPORTANT TERMS FOR SECTION III

**Completion:** Fill in the blanks to complete the definitions of key terms for this section of Chapter 2.

1. **scientific method:** System of established principles and processes of scientific inquiry, including identification of a problem to be studied, formulation and testing of alternative _____, collection and analysis of data, and public dissemination of findings so that other scientists can check, learn from, analyze, repeat, and build on the results.

2. **sample:** Group of participants chosen to _____ the entire population under study.

3. **random selection:** Sampling method that ensures representativeness because each member of the _____ has an equal and independent chance to be selected.

4. _____ **observation:** Research method in which behavior is studied in _____ settings without the observer's intervention or manipulation.

5. _____ **observation:** Research method in which the behavior of all participants is noted and recorded in the same situation, under controlled conditions.

6. **observer** _____: Tendency of an observer to misinterpret or distort data to fit his or her expectations.

7. **case study:** Scientific study covering a single case or life, based on notes taken by observers or on published _____ materials.

8. **correlational study:** Research design intended to discover whether a statistical relationship between variables exists, either in _____ or in magnitude.

9. **experiment:** Rigorously controlled, _____ (repeatable) procedure in which the researcher manipulates variables to assess the effect of one on the other.

10. **experimental group:** In an experiment, the group receiving the treatment under study; any changes in these people are compared with changes in the _____ group.

11. _____ **group:** In an experiment, a group of people who are similar to the people in the experimental group but who do not receive the treatment whose effects are to be measured; the results obtained with this group are compared with the results obtained with the experimental group.

12. _____ **variable:** In an experiment, the condition over which the experimenter has direct control.

13. _____ **variable:** In an experiment, the condition that may or may not change as a result of changes in the _____ variable.

14. _____ **assignment:** Technique used in assigning members of a study sample to experimental and control groups, in which each member of the sample has an equal chance to be assigned to each group and to receive or not receive the treatment.

15. _____ **study:** Study design in which data are collected about the same people over a period of time, to assess developmental changes that occur with age.

16. _____ **study:** Study design in which people of different ages are assessed on one occasion, providing comparative information about different age cohorts.

17. **cross-sequential study:** Study design that combines sequential and longitudinal techniques by assessing people in a _____ sample more than once.

## LEARNING OBJECTIVES FOR SECTION III

After reading and reviewing this section of Chapter 2, you should be able to do the following. (Remember: When you are asked to give examples, try to think of examples other than those given in the text.)

1.   State the five steps in the scientific method.

2.   Explain how and why researchers select a random sample.

3.   Name three basic types of data collection and tell advantages and disadvantages of each.

4.   Explain the uses and limitations of case studies, correlational studies, and experiments.

5.  Explain why experimenters may randomly assign participants in an experiment to experimental and control groups.

6.  Name three types of experiments, and tell the two major ways in which they differ.

7.  Compare the advantages and disadvantages of sequential, longitudinal, and cross-sequential designs.

8.  Identify three ethical principles that guide research on child development, and explain three important concerns about the rights of participants.

## CHAPTER 2 QUIZ

**Matching**--Who's Who: Match each person at the left with the appropriate description on the right.

1. Albert Bandura _____

2. Sigmund Freud _____

3. Erik Erikson _____

4. U. Bronfenbrenner _____

5. Ivan Pavlov _____

6. John B. Watson _____

7. G. Stanley Hall _____

8. Jean Piaget _____

9. B. F. Skinner _____

10. Alfred Binet _____

11. Margaret Mead _____

12. Charles Darwin _____

13. Lev Vygotsky _____

14. Maria Montessori _____

a. German-born psychologist who expanded on Freud's theory to emphasize the role of society in personality development

b. Russian physiologist who studied classical conditioning

c. American psychologist who formulated principles of social-learning theory

d. American psychologist who originated the ecological approach to understanding influences on development

e. First psychologist to formulate a theory of adolescence

f. French psychologist who developed the first individual intelligence test

g. Swiss theoretician, famous for his observations of children and his theory of cognitive stages of development

h. Originator of psychoanalytic perspective

i. American behavioral psychologist who applied stimulus-response theories of learning to child development

j. American psychologist who formulated basic principles of operant conditioning

k. Russian psychologist who originated sociocultural theory

l. World famous American anthropologist

m. Italian physician who developed a method of early childhood education

n. English naturalist. Originated the theory of evolution

**Multiple-Choice:** Circle the choice that best completes or answers each item.

1. According to diaries of going back to the sixteenth century, parents in those days
   a. treated children as miniature adults
   b. subjected children to harsh discipline and abuse
   c. were concerned about weaning and teething
   d. took children's illness or death in stride, since it was so common

2. The goals of child development as a discipline include all but which of the following?
   a. description
   b. explanation
   c. prediction
   d. compensation

3. The organismic model of development sees people as
   a. machines
   b. active initiators of development
   c. reactors to external forces
   d. blank slates

4. According to Freud's theory, the chief source of pleasure during the phallic stage is the
   a. mouth
   b. anus
   c. genitals
   d. superego

5. In Bronfenbrenner's terminology, the interlocking systems that contain the developing child compose the
   a. microsystem
   b. mesosystem
   c. exosystem
   d. macrosystem

6. In Freud's theory, the id is
   a. present at birth
   b. not developed until infants recognize that they are separate beings
   c. replaced by the ego
   d. a source of gratification

7. The "reality principle" refers to the
   a. superego
   b. ego
   c. id
   d. defense mechanisms

8. In Erikson's theory, the "virtue" developed during infancy is
   a. trust
   b. hope
   c. attachment
   d. obedience

9. Learning theories stress
   a. cognitive stages
   b. developmental changes
   c. hereditary influences
   d. environmental influences

10. The learning perspective includes
    a. cognitive-stage theory
    b. sociocultural theory
    c. behaviorism
    d. information-processing approach

11. In operant conditioning, negative reinforcement is
    a. withdrawal of a privilege
    b. withdrawal of an aversive event
    c. another term for punishment
    d. generally ineffective

12. Social-learning theory regards the learner as
    a. active
    b. molded by the environment
    c. influenced mainly by maturation
    d. influenced mainly by reinforcement and punishment

13. The term scheme is associated with
    a. Sigmund Freud
    b. Erik Erikson
    c. Jean Piaget
    d. Lev Vygotsky

14. Which of the following is a neo-Piagetian theorist?
    a. Jean Baker Miller
    b. Robbie Case
    c. Alfred Binet
    d. John Dewey

15. Cindy, age 8, has almost mastered the multiplication tables but is having trouble with some combinations. According to Vygotsky's theory, her parents should:
    a. insist on daily practice, and test her until she gets a perfect score
    b. leave her alone, since she will learn on her own when she is ready
    c. give plenty of praise to build her self-esteem
    d. give hints and ask leading questions to help her get the answers she can't get by herself

16.. All but which of the following are self-reports?
   a. diary
   b. interview
   c. questionnaire
   d. blood test
17. A correlation describes
   a. cause and effect
   b. direction and magnitude of a relationship between variables
   c. practical implications of a relationship between variables
   d. which variable in an experiment is dependent and which is independent
18. Which of the following can be used to establish a causal relationship?
   a. case study
   b. laboratory observation
   c. experiment
   d. any of the above
19. Which kind of experiment can be used to study environmental effects on identical twins separated at birth?
   a. laboratory experiment
   b. field experiment
   c. natural experiment
   d. none of the above; experimentation on human beings is unethical
20. A drawback of longitudinal research is
   a. attrition
   b. confounding developmental effects with cohort effects
   c. tendency for participants to do more poorly in later tests
   d. tendency to mask individual differences

**True or False?** In the blank following each item, write T (for true) or F (for false). In the space below each item, if the statement is false, rewrite it to make it true.

1. According to Bronfenbrenner's ecological approach, the effect upon a child of the parent's divorce is part of the child's exosytem. _____

2. A theory is information obtained through research. _____

3. A hypothesis is a prediction that can be tested by research. _____

4. Behavioral genetics has shown that intelligence is almost entirely inherited. _____

5. In Freud's theory, the superego operates under the reality principle. _____

6. Erikson's theory is based on Piaget's. _____

7. According to Erikson, successful resolution of each crisis requires discarding a negative trait in order to acquire the corresponding positive trait. _____

8. The learning perspective sees change as qualitative. _____

9. Learning theorists see development as occurring in clearly defined stages _____.

10. In classical conditioning, an unconditioned stimulus automatically elicits an unlearned response. _____

11. Reinforcement is a crucial element in classical conditioning. _____

12. According to social-learning theory, children develop abilities through observing and imitating models. _____

13. According to Piaget, accommodation and assimilation are both forms of adaptation. _____

14 .Information-processing researchers ask children to recall lists of words. _____

15. Neo-Piagetian psychologists combine elements of Piaget's theory with the ethological approach. _____

16. John Bowlby's convictions about the importance of the mother-baby bond were based on studies of animals and clinically disturbed children. _____

17. Human beings mature more rapidly than other primates. _____

18. Both naturalistic observation and laboratory observation are subject to observer bias. _____

19. Tests based on Vygotsky's concept of the of proximal development focus on children's potential, rather than actual, development. _____

20. Random sampling is the best way to assign participants to groups in an experiment. _____

# ANSWER KEY FOR CHAPTER 2

**CHAPTER 2 REVIEW**

**Important Terms for Section I**
1. explain/predict
3. explanations
4. stimuli
5. different

**Important Terms for Section II**
1. psychoanalytic
2. gratification
3. pleasure
4. reality
5. identification
6. Erikson
7. hope
8. adaptation
9. experience
10. predictable
11. learning
12. reinforced
13. increases
14. decreases
15. models
16. observational
17. cognitive
18. system
19. schemes
20. complementary
21. assimilation
22. accommodation
23. equilibration
24. information, information
25. evolutionary
26. social
27. Vygotsky
28. proximal, ZPD
29. microsystem

**Important Terms for Section III**
1. hypotheses
2. represent
3. population
4. naturalistic, natural
5. laboratory
6. bias
7. biographical
8. direction
9. replicable

10. control
11. control
12. independent
13. dependent, independent
14. random
15. longitudinal
16. cross-sectional
17. cross-sectional

**CHAPTER 2 QUIZ**

**Matching--Who's Who**
1. c
2. h
3. a
4. d
5. b
6. i
7. e
8. g
9. j
10. f
11. l
12. n
13. k
14. m

**Multiple-Choice**
1. b
2. d
3. b
4. c
5. b
6. a
7. b
8. b

9. d

10. c

11. b

12. a

13. c

14. b

15. d

16. d

17. b

18. c

19. c

20. b

16. T

17. F-Human beings mature more slowly than other primates.

18. T

19. T

20. F-Random assignment is the best way to assign participants to groups in an experiment.

## True or False?

In the blank following each item, write T (for true) or F (for false). In the space below each item, if the statement is false, rewrite it to make it true.

1. F-The effect of the parents' divorce is part of the child's microsystem.

2. F-A theory is an attempt to organize and explain information obtained through research.

3. T

4. F-Behavioral genetics has shown that intelligence has a strong hereditary component, but environment also has an influence.

5. F-The ego operates under the reality principle; the superego represents socially approved values.

6. F-Erikson's theory is based on Freud's.

7. F-Successful resolution requires a balance between a positive trait and a negative one.

8. F-The learning perspective emphasizes quantitative change.

9. F-Learning theorists do not describe stages of development.

10. T

11. F-Reinforcement is an element of operant conditioning.

12. T

13. T

14. T

15. F-Neo-Piagetian psychologists combine elements of Piaget's theory with the information-processing approach.

# FORMING A NEW LIFE: CONCEPTION, HEREDITY, AND ENVIRONMENT

## OVERVIEW

Chapter 3 traces the earliest development of a child, beginning with the parents' decision to conceive. In this chapter, the authors:

❑ Discuss why and when people choose to have children

❑ Describe human reproduction and explain how a new human life is created

❑ Identify causes and treatments of infertility, and describe alternative ways for infertile couples to become parents

❑ Explain the genetic mechanisms through which offspring inherit characteristics from parents

❑ Explain genetic transmission of various types of birth defects and discuss how genetic counseling and prenatal diagnosis can help parents who are worried about bearing a child with such a defect

❑ Discuss the relative influences of heredity and environment and how these factors work together

## GUIDEPOSTS FOR STUDY

3.1   How does conception normally occur and how have beliefs about conception changed?

3.2   What causes multiple births?

3.3   What causes infertility and what are alternative ways of becoming parents?

3.4   What genetic mechanisms determine sex, physical appearance, and other characteristics?

3.5   How are birth defects and other disorders transmitted?

3.6   How do scientists study the relative influences of heredity and environment and how do heredity and environment work together?

3.7   What roles do heredity and environment play in physical health, intelligence, and  personality?

## CHAPTER 3 REVIEW

**Section I  Becoming Parents**

FRAMEWORK FOR SECTION I

A.      Conception
   1.  Changing Ideas about Conception
   2.  How Fertilization Takes Place

B.      What Causes Multiple Births?

C.      Infertility

## IMPORTANT TERMS FOR SECTION I

**Completion:** Fill in the blanks to complete the definitions of key terms for this section of Chapter 3.

1. _____: Union of sperm and ovum to produce a zygote; also called <u>conception.</u>

2. **zygote:** One-celled organism resulting from _____.

3. **dizygotic (two-egg) twins:** Twins conceived by the union of two different ova (or a single ovum that has split) with two different sperm cells within a brief period of time; also called _____ twins.

4. **monozygotic (one-egg) twins:** Twins resulting from the division of a single zygote after fertilization; also called _____ twins.

5. _____: Person's characteristic disposition or style of approaching and reacting to situations.

6. _____: Inability to conceive after 12 to 18 months of trying.

7. **artificial insemination:** Injection of sperm into a woman's _____ in order to enable her to conceive.

8. _____ **fertilization:** Fertilization of an ovum outside the mother's body.

9. **ovum** _____: Method of fertilization in which a woman who cannot produce normal ova receives an ovum donated by fertile women.

10. _____ **motherhood:** Method of conception in which a woman who is not married to a man agrees to bear his baby and then give the child to the father and his mate.

11. _____: a genetic copy of an individual.

## LEARNING OBJECTIVES FOR SECTION I

After reading and reviewing this section of Chapter 3, you should be able to do the following.

1. Explain why deciding whether or not to have children is more complicated today than it was in preindustrial times.

2. Describe what happens during ovulation and fertilization.

3. Explain the difference between monozygotic and dizygotic twins and cite factors affecting the incidence of each.

4. Give at least three common causes of infertility in men and in women, and mention three common treatments.

5. Describe four methods of assisted reproduction and point out some of the ethical questions involved.

6. Define cloning and discuss some ethical considerations involved.

**Section II  Mechanisms of Heredity**

FRAMEWORK FOR SECTION II

A.      The Genetic code

B.      What Determines Sex?

C.      Patterns of Genetic Transmission
  1.    Dominant and Recessive Inheritance
  2.    Genotypes and Phenotypes: Multifactorial Transmission

D.      Genetic and Chromosomal Abnormalities
  1.    Defects Transmitted by Dominant or Recessive Inheritance
  2.    Defects Transmitted by Sex-Linked Inheritance

3. Genome Imprinting
4. Chromosomal Abnormalities
5. Genome Imprinting

E.      Genetic Counseling and Testing

## IMPORTANT TERMS FOR SECTION II

**Completion:** Fill in the blanks to complete the definitions of key terms for this section of Chapter 3.

1. _____: Basic functional unit of heredity that contains all inherited material passed from biological parents to children.

2. **deoxyribonucleic acid (DNA):** Chemical of which genes are composed that controls the _____/_____ of body cells.

3. _____: One of 46 rod-shaped structures that carry the genes.

4. _____: The 22 pairs of chromosomes not related to sexual expression.

5. **sex chromosomes:** Pair of chromosomes that determines sex: XX in the normal female, _____ in the normal male.

6. _____: Paired genes (alike or different) that affect a particular trait.

7. **homozygous:** Possessing two _____ alleles for a trait.

8. **heterozygous:** Possessing _____ alleles for a trait.

9. **dominant inheritance:** Pattern of inheritance in which, when an individual receives contradictory alleles for a trait, only the dominant one is _____.

10. **recessive inheritance:** Pattern of inheritance in which an individual receives _____ recessive alleles from both parents, resulting in expression of a recessive (nondominant) trait.

11. _____ **inheritance:** Interaction of several sets of genes to produce a complex trait.

12. _____ **transmission:** Combination of genetic and environmental factors to produce certain complex traits.

13. **phenotype:** _____ characteristics of a person.

14. _____: Genetic makeup of a person, containing both expressed and unexpressed characteristics.

15. **sex-linked inheritance:** Pattern of inheritance in which certain characteristics carried on the _____ chromosome inherited from the mother are transmitted differently to her male and female offspring.

16. **Down syndrome:** Chromosomal disorder characterized by moderate-to-severe mental _____ and by such physical signs as a downward-sloping skin fold at the inner corners of the eyes.

17. _____ **counseling:** Clinical service that advises couples of their probable risk of having children with particular hereditary defects.

18. _____ **testing:** Procedure for ascertaining a person's _____ makeup for purposes of identifying predispositions to specific hereditary diseases or disorders.

## LEARNING OBJECTIVES FOR SECTION II

After reading and reviewing this section of Chapter 3, you should be able to do the following.

1. Tell what genes do and explain the significance of their location on the chromosomes.

2. Distinguish between meiosis and mitosis and between monomorphic and polymorphic genes.

3. Explain how the sex of a child is determined, and how and when an embryo develops male or female characteristics.

4. Contrast dominant and recessive inheritance and explain how each occurs.

5. Tell why most normal traits are not the result of simple dominant or recessive transmission?

6. Explain how a person can be either homozygous or heterozygous for an expressed trait.

7. Explain the difference between a person's phenotype and that person's genotype, and give an example.

8. Describe three methods of inheritance of defects, and give at least one example of each.

9. Explain why defects transmitted by dominant inheritance tend to be less deadly early in life than those transmitted recessively.

10. Name two ways in which chromosomal abnormalities can occur.

11. Identify the causes and characteristics of Down syndrome and discuss the outlook for a child born with this disorder.

12. Tell how genome imprinting occurs and give an example of its effect.

13. Tell how a genetic counselor assesses the probability that a child will be born with an inherited defect.

14. Discuss the benefits and risks of genetic testing.

## Section III Nature and Nurture: Influences of Heredity and Environment

### FRAMEWORK FOR SECTION III

A. Studying the Relative Influences of Heredity and Environment
1. Measuring Heritability
2. Effects of the Prenatal Environment

B. How Heredity and Environment Work Together
1. Reaction Range and Canalization
2. Genotype-Environment Interaction
3. Genotype-Environment Correlation
4. What Makes Siblings So Different? The Nonshared Environment

C. Some Characteristics Influenced by Heredity and Environment
1. Physical and Physiological Traits
2. Intelligence and School Achievement
3. Personality
4. Psychopathology

### IMPORTANT TERMS FOR SECTION III

**Completion:** Fill in the blanks to complete the definitions of key terms for this section of Chapter 3.

1. **behavioral genetics:** Quantitative study of relative genetic and environmental _____ on behavioral and psychological traits.

2. **heritability:** Statistical estimate of contribution of heredity to individual differences in a specific _____ within a given population.

3. **concordant:** Term describing _____ who share the same trait or disorder.

4. _____: Potential variability, depending on environmental conditions, in the expression of a hereditary trait.

5. _____: Limitation on variance of expression pf certain inherited characteristics.

6. **genotype-environment** _____: The portion of phenotypic variation that results from the reactions of genetically different individuals to similar environmental conditions.

7. **genotype-environment** _____: Tendency of certain genetic and environmental influences to occur together; may be passive, reactive (evocative), or active. Also called genotype-environment covariance.

8. _____-picking: Tendency of a person, especially after early childhood, to seek out environments compatible with his or her genotype.

9. _____ environmental effects: The unique environment in which each child grows up, consisting of dissimilar influences or influences that affect each child differently.

10. **obesity:** Extreme overweight in relation to age, sex, height, and body type; sometimes defined as having a _____ (weight-for-height) at or above the 85th percentile of growth curves for children of the same age and sex.

11. **autism:** One of a group of pervasive developmental disorders (PDD) of the brain that develops within the first 2½ years and is characterized by lack of sociability, impaired _____, and a narrow range of repetitive, often obsessive behaviors.

## LEARNING OBJECTIVES FOR SECTION III

After reading and reviewing this section of Chapter 3, you should be able to do the following.

1. Tell how researchers determine the heritability of a trait.

2. Describe three common types of studies of the influences of hereditary and environmental factors in development.

3. Explain the concepts of reaction range and canalization, and give at least one example of each.

4. Give an example of genotype-environment interaction.

5. Define and give examples of three types of genotype-environment correlation.

6. Explain why siblings tend to be more different than alike in intellect and personality, and why each experiences a unique environment within the family.

7. Assess the influences of heredity and environment on obesity, longevity, intelligence, personality traits, temperament, shyness and boldness.

8. Identify the characteristics and probable causes of schizophrenia and autism.

# CHAPTER 3 QUIZ

**Matching--Numbers:** Match each item at the left with the correct number in the right-hand column. (Note: A number may be used more than once.)

1. Number of days in the female ovulation cycle _____

2. Approximate percentage of American couples who experience infertility _____

3. Maximum estimated success rate for in vitro fertilization (percent) _____

4. Number of chromosomes in sex cells (gametes) _____

5. Percentage of offspring of hybrid pea plants showing the dominant trait in Mendel's cross-breeding experiments _____

6. Approximate percentage of babies born in the United States who have birth defects _____

7. Number of the chromosome associated with Down syndrome _____

8. Maximum percentage of heritability for most traits _____

a.  6

b.  8

c.  75

d.  20

e.  21

f.  50

g.  28

h.  46

**Multiple-Choice:** Circle the choice that best completes or answers each item.

1. Having a first child in the thirties is
   a. most common among women who have not finished high school
   b. more common today than having a first child in the twenties
   c. riskier than was previously believed
   d. none of the above

2. Fertilization normally occurs in the
   a. uterus
   b. vagina
   c. cervix
   d. fallopian tube

3. A newborn girl has approximately how many immature ova in her ovaries?
   a. none
   b. 40
   c. 4000
   d. 400,000

4. The incidence of multiple births has been increasing because of
   a. increased use of fertility drugs
   b. increased rate of sexual activity
   c. aftereffects of birth control pills
   d. none of the above; such births are accidental

5. The most common cause of male infertility is
   a. low sperm count
   b. inability to ejaculate
   c. blocked passage for sperm
   d. low mobility of sperm

6. In vitro fertilization is
   a. a form of artificial insemination
   b. conception outside the body
   c. successful in at least one-third of cases
   d. still in the experimental stage

7. The chemical called DNA
   a. tells the cells how to manufacture proteins that control body functions
   b. tells the cells to produce testosterone
   c. causes a fetus to develop female body parts
   d. causes chromosomal abnormalities

8. A genetically male zygote can result from which combination of sex chromosomes?
   a. YY
   b. XY
   c. XX
   d. any of the above

9. Which of the following statements about genes is true?
   a. Each gene acts independently of other genes in determining a trait.
   b. Each cell in the human body contains approximately 10,000 genes.
   c. Three-fourths of the genes a child receives are identical to those received by every other child.
   d. Genes are made of proteins.
10. Mendel's experiments proved that
    a. Traits are transmitted independently of each other.
    b. All inherited traits are expressed.
    c. Most traits are inherited polygenically.
    d. Most traits are inherited multifactorially.
11. The pattern of alleles underlying a person's observable traits is called his or her
    a. karyotype
    b. prototype
    c. phenotype
    d. genotype
12. Birth disorders account for approximately what percentage of deaths in infancy?
    a. less than 1 percent
    b. 5 percent
    c. 10 percent
    d. more than 20 percent
13. African Americans are at higher-than-average risk of carrying genes for
    a. sickle-cell anemia
    b. Tay-Sachs disease
    c. cystic fibrosis
    d. beta thalassemia
14. Chromosomal abnormalities are the result of
    a. inheritance
    b. prenatal accidents
    c. either a or b
    d. neither a nor b
15. Genome imprinting is
    a. a form of sex-linked inheritance
    b. a form of recessive inheritance
    c. apparently involved in Huntington's disease
    d. the result of a permanent mutation

16. The Human Genome Project is designed to
    a. map the location of genes and identify those that cause disorders
    b. conduct genetic tests to identify people who carry harmful genes
    c. perform gene therapy to repair abnormal genes
    d. counsel couples on their risk of having a child with a birth defect
17. Genetic determinism is
    a. another term for heritability.
    b. a reason for concern about genetic testing.
    c. a view supported by Sandra Scarr
    d. a basic principle of behavioral genetics.
18. Which of the following is a method of studying relative effects of heredity and environment?
    a. correlational study
    b. adoption study
    c. case study
    d. cross-sequential study
19. A human characteristic that is highly canalized is
    a. body size
    b. eye color
    c. rate of language development
    d. shyness
20. Which of the following is an example of genotype-environment interaction?
    a. Sarah is taller than her parents because she has a better diet than they did as children.
    b. Maria learned to talk earlier than her sister Julia because her parents spent more time talking to her as an infant.
    c. Wendell has a higher IQ than his identical twin brother Mitch, who was adopted at birth.
    d. Selena, who was born with the PKU gene, will be mentally retarded unless put on a special diet.
21. Mia's parents sent her to a tennis camp because she showed an aptitude for the sport. This is an example of
    a. passive correlation
    b. reactive correlation
    c. active correlation
    d. niche-picking

22. Which of the following statements about heredity and intelligence is true?
    a. Intelligence is controlled by a few specific genes.
    b. The influence of heredity on intelligence diminishes with age.
    c. The prenatal environment seems to have an important impact on intelligence.
    d. Because of the strength of genetic influences on intelligence, little can be done to improve IQ scores.

23. Shyness
    a. is largely inborn
    b. occurs with similar frequency in all cultures
    c. is unaffected by parental treatment
    d. is more common in adopted children than in children living with their biological parents

**True or False?** In the blank following each item, write T (for true) or F (for false). In the space below each item, if the statement is false, rewrite it to make it true.

1. In preindustrial societies, large families were rare. _____

2. The ovum is the largest cell in the adult human body. _____

3. A sperm may locate a fertile ovum by its scent. _____

4. Twins are always of the same sex. _____

5. About 20 percent of infertile couples eventually conceive_____

6. Ovum transfer can help a postmenopausal woman bear a child. _____

7. Every cell in the human body has 46 chromosomes (23 pairs). _____

8. Mitosis is a process of cell division normally resulting in exact duplicates of the original cell. _____

9. The father's sperm normally determines a child's sex. _____

10. Twenty-two of the twenty-three pairs of chromosomes are autosomes. _____

11. Most normal human traits can be explained by Mendel's law of dominant inheritance. _____

12. Skin color is an example of polygenic inheritance. _____

13. Multifactorial transmission is the result of the interaction of several different genes. _____

14. Normal genes are usually dominant over abnormal ones. _____

15. If a couple's first child has a recessive defect, the second child will also have it. _____

16. Red-green color blindness is a sex-linked trait. _____

17. Dennis has hemophilia. His son, Ira, has a 50 percent chance of inheriting the abnormal gene and being a carrier of the disorder. _____

18. The risk of Down syndrome rises with the age of either parent. _____

19. Family (kinship) studies provide a good way to distinguish hereditary from environmental influences. _____

20. If dizygotic twins are highly concordant for a trait, the trait is likely to be strongly influenced by heredity. _____

21. Stunted growth due to malnutrition is an example of reaction range. _____

22. Maturation is programmed by the genes and cannot be affected by environmental factors. _____

23. Differences in personalities of siblings who grow up in the same household are due to genetic differences. _____

24. Temperament is mostly the result of parental responsiveness during early infancy. _____

25. Schizophrenia appears to be transmitted multifactorially. _____

# ANSWER KEY FOR CHAPTER 3

## CHAPTER 3 REVIEW

### Important Terms for Section I

1. fertilization
2. fertilization
3. fraternal
4. identical
5. temperament
6. infertility
7. cervix
8. in vitro
9. transfer
10. surrogate
11. clone

### Important Terms for Section II

1. gene
2. functions/formation
3. chromosome
4. autosomes
5. XY
6. alleles
7. identical
8. differing
9. expressed
10. identical
11. polygenic
12. multifactorial
13. observable
14. genotype
15. X
16. retardation
17. genetic
18. genetic, genetic

### Important Terms for Section III

1. influences
2. trait
3. twins
4. reaction range
5. canalization
6. interaction
7. correlation
8. niche
9. nonshared
10. body mass index
11. communication

## CHAPTER 3 QUIZ

### Matching--Numbers

1. g
2. b
3. d
4. h
5. c
6. a
7. e
8. f

### Multiple-Choice

1. d
2. d
3. d
4. a
5. a
6. b
7. a
8. b
9. c
10. a
11. d
12. d
13. a
14. c
15. c
16. a
17. b
18. b
19. b
20. d
21. b
22. c
23. a

### True or False?

1. F-In preindustrial societies, large families served economic and social needs.
2. T
3. T
4. F-Monozygotic twins are of the same sex, but dizygotic twins may be of the same sex or different sexes.
5. F-About 50 percent of infertile couples eventually conceive.
6. T

7. F-Every cell in the human body except the sex cells has 46 chromosomes; the sex cells have 23 chromosomes.
8. T
9. T
10. T
11. F-Hardly any normal human traits are transmitted by simple dominant inheritance.
12. T
13. F-Multifactorial transmission is the result of the interaction of genetic and environmental factors.
14. T
15. F-The child will not necessarily have the defect; each child of a man and woman who carry a gene for a recessive defect has a 1 in 4 chance of inheriting the defect.
16. T
17. F-A man cannot pass on the gene for hemophilia to his son, because it is carried on the X chromosome.
18. T
19. F-Family studies alone do not clearly distinguish hereditary from environmental influences.
20. F-If monozygotic twins are more concordant than dizygotic twins for a trait, the trait is likely to be strongly influenced by heredity.
21. T
22. F-Environmental factors can affect the pace and timing of maturation.
23. F-Differences among siblings are due in part to nonshared environmental effects.
24. F-Temperament appears to be largely inborn.
25. T

# CHAPTER 4
# PREGNANCY AND PRENATAL DEVELOPMENT

## OVERVIEW

Chapter 4 explores the development of the child from conception to birth. In this chapter, the authors:

❑ Outline three stages of prenatal development

❑ Describe the developing capabilities of the fetus

❑ Discuss environmental hazards that can affect the fetus

❑ Describe prenatal assessment techniques and explain the importance of prenatal care

## GUIDEPOSTS FOR STUDY

4.1 What are the three stages of prenatal development and what happens during each stage?

4.2 What can fetuses do?

4.3 What environmental influences can affect prenatal development?

4.4 What techniques can assess a fetus' health and well-being and what is the importance of prenatal care?

## CHAPTER 4 REVIEW

**Section I Prenatal Development : Three Stages**

FRAMEWORK FOR SECTION I

A.     Germinal Stage (Fertilization to 2 Weeks)

B.     Embryonic Stage (2 to 8 Weeks)

C.     Fetal Stage (8 Weeks to Birth)

IMPORTANT TERMS FOR SECTION I

**Completion:** Fill in the blanks to complete the definitions of key terms for this section of Chapter 4.

1. **gestation:** The approximately _____-day period of development between fertilization and birth.

2. _____ **principle:** Principle that development proceeds in a head-to-toe direction (i.e., that upper parts of the body develop before lower parts).

3. _____ **principle:** Principle that development proceeds from within to without (i.e., that parts of the body near the center develop before the extremities).

4. _____ **stage:** First 2 weeks of prenatal development, characterized by rapid cell division, increasing complexity and differentiation, and implantation in the wall of the uterus.

5. _____ **stage:** Second stage of gestation (2 to 8 weeks), characterized by rapid growth and development of major body systems and organs.

6. **spontaneous abortion:** Natural expulsion from the uterus of an embryo or fetus that cannot survive outside the womb; also called _____.

7. _____ **stage:** Final stage of gestation (from 8 weeks to birth), characterized by increased detail of body parts and greatly enlarged body size.

8. _____: Prenatal medical procedure using high-frequency _____ waves to detect the outline of a fetus and its movements, so as to determine whether a pregnancy is progressing normally.

## LEARNING OBJECTIVES FOR SECTION I

After reading and reviewing this section of Chapter 4, you should be able to do the following.

1. Tell how the cephalocaudal and proximodistal principles apply to prenatal development, and give examples.

2. Summarize the development that occurs during the germinal stage.

3. Define the following terms: blastocyst, embryonic disk, ectoderm, endoderm, mesoderm, placenta, umbilical cord, amniotic sac, and trophoblast.

4. Identify three functions of the placenta.

5. Explain why the embryonic stage is considered a critical period.

6. Summarize the development that occurs during the embryonic stage.

7. Explain why some pregnancies terminate in spontaneous abortion, what factors increase the risk of spontaneous abortion, and what complications may occur.

8. Give three possible reasons why males are more vulnerable during the prenatal period and throughout life.

9. Summarize the development that takes place during the fetal stage.

10. Describe the fetal environment and explain how it affects fetal activity and development.

11. Discuss individual and gender differences in fetal activity and temperament.

12. Summarize findings about fetal sensory and cognitive abilities.

## Section II Prenatal Development: Environmental Influences
### FRAMEWORK FOR SECTION II

A.   Maternal Factors

B.   Physical Activity

C.   Drug Intake
   1.   Medical Drugs
   2.   Alcohol
   3.   Nicotine
   4.   Caffeine
   5.   Marijuana, Opiates, and Cocaine

D.   Sexually Transmitted Diseases and Other Maternal Illnesses

E.   Maternal Age

F.   Outside Environmental Hazards

G.   Paternal Factors

## IMPORTANT TERMS FOR SECTION II

**Completion:** Fill in the blanks to complete the definitions of key terms for this section of Chapter 4.

   1. **teratogenic:** Capable of causing birth _____.

2. _____ _____ _____ (abbreviated _____ ): Combination of mental, motor, and developmental abnormalities affecting the offspring of some women who drink heavily during pregnancy.

3. **acquired immune deficiency syndrome (AIDS):** Viral disease that undermines effective _____ of the immune system.

## LEARNING OBJECTIVES FOR SECTION II

After reading and reviewing this section of Chapter 4, you should be able to do the following.

1. Tell how researchers study prenatal hazards.

2. Discuss factors to be weighed in considering the issue of fetal rights.

3. Identify factors in good nutrition during pregnancy, and assess the value of dietary supplements.

4. Summarize expert recommendations regarding exercise during pregnancy.

5. Explain how drug intake during pregnancy can harm an embryo or fetus, and discuss effects of medical drugs, alcohol, nicotine, caffeine, marijuana, opiates, and cocaine.

6. Tell how a fetus can contract HIV infection from the mother and how transmission can be prevented, and discuss the prospects for children born with HIV.

7. Name at least three other illnesses that can be passed from mother to fetus and describe their consequences.

8. Assess the risks of complications for expectant mothers over the age of 30.

9. Identify prenatal risks involved in exposure to industrial chemicals, lead contamination, and radiation.

10. Identify several ways in which a man can contribute to the risk of birth defects in his child.

**Section III Monitoring Prenatal Development**

## IMPORTANT TERMS FOR SECTION III

**Completion:** Fill in the blanks to complete the definitions of the key terms for this section of Chapter 4.

1. **amniocentesis:** Prenatal diagnostic procedure in which a sample of _____ is withdrawn and analyzed to determine whether any of certain genetic defects are present.
2. **chorionic villus sampling (CVS):** Prenatal diagnostic procedure in which tissue from villi (hairlike projections of the _____ surrounding the fetus) is analyzed for birth defects.
3. _____: Prenatal medical procedure in which a scope is inserted in the abdomen of a pregnant woman to permit viewing of the embryo for diagnosis and treatment of abnormalities.
4. **preimplantation genetic diagnosis:** Medical procedure in which cells from an embryo conceived by ___ _____ _____ are analyzed for genetic defects prior to implantation of the embryo in the mother's uterus.
5. **umbilical cord sampling:** Prenatal medical procedure in which samples of a fetus's blood are taken from the umbilical cord to assess body functioning; also called _____ _____ _____.
6. **maternal blood test** Prenatal diagnostic procedure to detect the presence of fetal abnormalities, used particularly when the fetus is at risk of defects in the _____ _____ _____.

## LEARNING OBJECTIVES FOR SECTION III

After reading and reviewing this section of Chapter 4, you should be able to do the following.

1. List eight advances in prenatal assessment and care that seem likely to occur or continue during the twenty-first century?

2. List and describe seven techniques for prenatal diagnosis of defects of abnormalities.

3. List three techniques for correcting fetal disorders.

4. Discuss the importance of early prenatal care.

# CHAPTER 4 QUIZ

**Matching**--Month by Month: Match each month of gestation in the left-hand column with the appropriate description (a typical development during that month) in the right-hand column.

1. First month _____
2. Second month _____
3. Third month _____
4. Fourth month _____
5. Fifth month _____
6. Sixth month _____
7. Seventh month _____
8. Eighth month _____
9. Ninth month _____

a. Sex can first be easily determined.
b. First signs of individual personality appear.
c. Body begins to catch up to head, growing to same proportions as at birth.
d. Fetus stops growing.
e. Growth is more rapid than at any other time during prenatal or postnatal life.
f. Reflex patterns are fully developed.
g. Layer of fat begins developing over entire body.
h. Skin becomes sensitive enough to react to tactile stimulation.
i. Fetus is first able to hear.

**Multiple-Choice**: Circle the choice that best completes or answers each item.

1. Which of the following is an example of the cephalocaudal principle?
   a. At 2 months of gestation, an embryo's head is half the length of its body.
   b. An embryo's arms and legs develop before the fingers and toes.
   c. both a and b
   d. neither a nor b
2. Mitosis, or rapid cell division, begins within how many hours after fertilization?
   a. 2
   b. 12
   c. 24
   d. 36
3. A fertilized ovum moves from the
   a. uterus to the fallopian tube
   b. fallopian tube to the uterus
   c. ovary to the fallopian tube
   d. fallopian tube to the ovary
4. In which stage of prenatal development does an unborn baby float freely in the uterus?
   a. germinal
   b. embryonic
   c. fetal
   d. none of the above

5. Which of the following protects the unborn child?
   a. embryonic disk
   b. endoderm
   c. amniotic sac
   d. blastocyst
6. The placenta does all but which of the following?
   a. provides immunity
   b. produces hormones
   c. nourishes the fetus
   d. promotes cell division
7. Which of the following is (are) most likely to cause a spontaneous abortion?
   a. chromosomal abnormalities
   b. uterine abnormalities
   c. defective sperm
   d. infection
8. Which of the following hypotheses has been advanced to explain why male babies are more vulnerable to miscarriage and disorder than female babies?
   a. The Y chromosome contains genes which protect females against stress.
   b. The X chromosome contains harmful genes.
   c. The mechanisms for immunity in males are inferior.
   d. The male body develops earlier in the prenatal period than the female body.

9. The fetal stage is characterized by
   a. high risk of miscarriage
   b. less, but more vigorous, activity
   c. occurrence of developmental birth defects
   d. increasing heart rate
10. The uterine walls and amniotic sac
    a. restrain fetal movement
    b. stimulate fetal movement
    c. both a and b
    d. neither a nor b
11. Which statement about fetal learning is true, according to research?
    a. Newborns prefer male voices to female voices.
    b. Newborns recognize stories that were read to them before birth.
    c. Newborns cannot yet distinguish between the mother's voice and that of another woman.
    d. Newborns show no preferences that suggest fetal learning has taken place.
12. Babies are less at risk when their mothers gain approximately how many pounds during pregnancy?
    a. 10 to 15
    b. 16 to 20
    c. 22 to 46
    d. none of the above; there is no known correlation between the mother's weight gain and the health of the baby
13. Pregnant women need how many extra calories daily?
    a. about 200
    b. 300 to 500
    c. 800 or more
    d. none; extra calories may make the baby obese
14. Which of the following statements about fetal alcohol syndrome (FAS) is true?
    a. It affects about 1 infant in 2,000 in the United States.
    b. It is characterized by extreme passivity.
    c. In infancy, it can involve sleep disturbances and weak sucking.
    d. Although severe in early childhood, its effects rarely persist into adulthood.

15. Which of the following has not been found to be related to a mother's heavy smoking during pregnancy?
    a. facial abnormalities
    b. low birth weight
    c. poor respiratory functioning
    d. learning and behavior problems
16. The effects of which of the following, when ingested during pregnancy, are still in question?
    a. caffeine
    b. birth control pills
    c. DES
    d. codeine
17. The use of which of the following drugs by a mother during pregnancy has been linked to neurological problems?
    a. cocaine
    b. marijuana
    c. both a and b
    d. neither a nor b
18. "Cocaine babies" tend to be
    a. irritable
    b. lethargic
    c. either a or b
    d. neither a nor b
19. AIDS can be passed to an unborn child through the mother's
    a. amniotic fluid
    b. genes
    c. blood
    d. none of the above; AIDS can be passed only through sexual contact
20. Fetal exposure to which of the following can cause gene mutations?
    a. incompatible maternal blood type
    b. PCBs
    c. lead
    d. radiation
21. If a father is in his late thirties or older when his baby is conceived, the child may have an increased risk of
    a. jaundice
    b. stillbirth
    c. anemia
    d. birth defects

22. Which of the following procedures can disclose the sex of a fetus?
    a. ultrasound and amniocentesis
    b. ultrasound and chorionic villus sampling
    c. amniocentesis and umbilical cord sampling
    d. fetal blood sampling and alpha fetoprotein test

23. A technique that allows a doctor to draw blood from a fetus to diagnose the presence of certain disorders is
    a. chorionic villus sampling
    b. umbilical cord sampling
    c. alpha fetoprotein (AFP) test
    d. amniocentesis

24. Doctors can give fetuses blood transfusions through the
    a. placenta
    b. amniotic fluid
    c. uterine walls
    d. umbilical cord

25. A woman in which of the following countries is least likely to obtain early prenatal care?
    a. Spain
    b. Israel
    c. Ireland
    d. United States

**True or False?** In the blank following each item, write T (for true) or F (for false). In the space below the item, if the statement is false, rewrite it to make it true.

1. Prospective parents are likely to be aware of their unborn baby's sleep-wake cycle by the sixth month of pregnancy. _____

2. Normal full-term gestation is 360 days.
_____

3. It usually takes 1 week for the fertilized ovum to reach the uterus. _____

4. The embryonic disk differentiates into three layers from which the various parts of the body will develop. _____

5. Most developmental birth defects occur during the first trimester of pregnancy. _____

6. Male babies are stronger than female babies and more likely to survive. _____

7. Differences in fetal activity seem to indicate temperamental patterns that may continue into adulthood. _____

8. Research has shown that fetuses can hear.
_____

9. In many states, expectant mothers who took illegal drugs have been prosecuted for child abuse or for delivering a controlled substance to a minor. _____

10. Gaining too much weight during pregnancy is riskier than gaining too little. _____

11. Giving folic acid supplements to pregnant women can help prevent neural-tube defects. _____

12. Jogging, swimming, bicycling, or playing tennis is likely to overstrain a pregnant woman and endanger the fetus. _____

13. It is <u>not</u> safe for a pregnant woman to take aspirin. _____

14. Any ill effects on a child of drugs taken during pregnancy will show up at or soon after birth. _____

15. An expectant mother who takes as little as one alcoholic drink per day may harm the fetus. _____

16. Cutting down on smoking during pregnancy can increase the baby's birth weight. _____

17. Women addicted to opiates are likely to bear addicted babies. _____

18. A child born with HIV infection will develop AIDS within the first two years of life. _____

19. If a mother contracts German measles at any time during her pregnancy, her baby is almost certain to be born deaf or with heart defects. _____

20. Women who delay childbearing until their late thirties are more likely to have complications of pregnancy than younger mothers. _____

21. An unborn child can be harmed by the mother's smoking but not by the father's smoking.

_____

22. In England, a woman who became pregnant in the 1890s was fifty times as likely to die in childbirth as today. _____

23. Chorionic villus sampling can be performed earlier in a pregnancy than amniocentesis.

_____

24. In the United States, nearly 1 in 5 pregnant women does not receive prenatal care in the first three months. _____

# ANSWER KEY FOR CHAPTER 4

## CHAPTER 4 REVIEW

### Important Terms for Section I
1. 266
2. cephalocaudal
3. proximodistal
4. germinal
5. embryonic
6. miscarriage
7. fetal
8. ultrasound, sound

### Important Terms for Section II
1. defects
2. fetal alcohol syndrome (FAS)
3. functioning

### Important Terms for Section III
1. amniotic fluid
2. membrane
3. embryoscopy
4. in vitro fertilization
5. fetal blood sampling
6. central nervous system

## CHAPTER 4 QUIZ

### Matching--Month by Month
1. e
2. h
3. a
4. c
5. b
6. i
7. f
8. g
9. d

### Multiple-Choice
1. a
2. d
3. b
4. a
5. c
6. d
7. a
8. c
9. b
10. c
11. b
12. c
13. b
14. c
15. a
16. a
17. c
18. c
19. c
20. d
21. d
22. a
23. b
24. d
25. d

### True or False?
1. F-Prospective parents are likely to be aware of their unborn baby's sleep-wake cycle by the eighth month of gestation.
2. F-Normal full-term gestation is 266 days.
3. F-It normally takes 3 or 4 days for the fertilized ovum to reach the uterus.
4. T
5. T
6. F-Male babies are more vulnerable to death and disorders.
7. T
8. T
9. T
10. F-Gaining too little weight during pregnancy is riskier than gaining too much.
11. T
12. F-Regular, moderate exercise can contribute to a more comfortable pregnancy and an easier, safer delivery and seems to have no ill effects on the fetuses of healthy women.
13. T
14. F-The effects of some drugs, such as the synthetic hormone DES, may not show up for many years.
15. T
16. T
17. T
18. F-Some babies born with HIV infection develop AIDS within the first year or two, but others live for years with few or no apparent effects.
19. F-If a mother contracts German measles before the eleventh week of pregnancy, her baby is almost certain to be born deaf and to have heart defects.
20. T

21. F-The father's smoking is associated with lower birthweight and a greater likelihood of his child's contracting cancer.
22. T
23. T
24. T

# CHAPTER 5
# BIRTH AND THE NEWBORN BABY

## OVERVIEW

Chapter 5 begins with the drama of birth: the climax of fetal development and the curtain raiser on child development in the world outside the womb. In this chapter, the authors:

❏ Describe what happens during the four stages of childbirth

❏ Discuss the pros and cons of various methods of, and alternative settings for, childbirth

❏ Describe the physical characteristics of a newborn baby and the changes in functioning that occur after the cutting of the umbilical cord

❏ Discuss potential complications of childbirth, including low birthweight, postmaturity, and stillbirth

❏ Tell how electronic fetal monitoring, the Agar scale, the Brazelton scale, and other screening instruments are used to check health and functioning during birth and the neonatal period

❏ Discuss whether there is a critical time for bonding between infants and parents

❏ Describe the typical alternation of newborns' states of arousal and how they change during infancy

❏ Discuss how the transition to parenthood affects marriage and family life

## GUIDEPOSTS FOR STUDY

5.1 How have customs surrounding birth changed?

5.2 How does labor begin, and what happens during each of the four stages of childbirth?

5.3 What alternative methods and settings of delivery are available today?

5.4 How do newborn infants adjust to life outside the womb?

5.5 How can we tell whether a new baby is healthy and is developing normally?

5.6 What complications of childbirth can endanger newborn babies and what can be done to enhance the chances of a positive outcome?

5.7 How do parents bond with their baby and respond to the baby's patterns of sleep and activity?

5.8 How does parenthood change the parents' relationship with one another?

## CHAPTER 5 REVIEW

### Section I   How Childbirth Has Changed

### Section II   The Birth Process

FRAMEWORK FOR SECTION I AND SECTION II

A.      Stages of Childbirth

B.      Methods of Delivery
    1.   Vaginal versus Cesarean Delivery
    2.   Medicated versus Unmediated Delivery

C.      Settings and Attendants for Childbirth

## IMPORTANT TERMS FOR SECTION I AND SECTION II

**Completion:**  Fill in the blanks to complete the definitions of key terms for this section of Chapter 5.

1. _____ **childbirth:** Method of childbirth, developed by Dr. Grantly Dick-Read, that seeks to prevent pain by eliminating the mother's fear of childbirth through education about the physiology of reproduction and training in methods of breathing and relaxation during delivery.

2. _____ **childbirth:** Method of childbirth, developed by Dr. Ferdinand Lamaze, that uses instruction, breathing exercises, and social support to induce controlled physical responses to uterine contractions and reduce fear and pain.

3. _____ **delivery:** Delivery of a baby by surgical removal from the uterus.

4. Hospitals are finding ways to _____ childbirth by providing a quiet homelike birthing room under soft lights, with the father present as a coach.


## LEARNING OBJECTIVES FOR SECTION I AND SECTION II

After reading and reviewing this section of Chapter 5, you should be able to do the following.

1. Describe how childbirth has changed over time.




2. Describe what occurs during each of the four stages of childbirth.




3. Discuss considerations that should enter into a woman's decision whether or not to have a medicated delivery.




4. State the principles of natural and prepared childbirth and briefly describe the Lamaze method.

5. Discuss some common reasons for and risks of cesarean delivery.

6. Discuss considerations in choosing whether to give birth in a hospital, at home, or in a birth center or maternity center, and in choosing attendance by a physician or a midwife.

## Section III  The Newborn Baby

### FRAMEWORK FOR SECTION III

A.    Size and Appearance
B.    Body Systems

### IMPORTANT TERMS FOR SECTION III

**Completion:**  Fill in the blanks to complete the definitions of key terms for this section of Chapter 5.

1. _____: Newborn baby, up to 4 weeks old.
2. _____ **period:** First 4 weeks of life, a time of transition from intrauterine dependency to independent existence.
3. **fontanels:** Soft spots on _____ of young infant.
4. **lanugo:** Fuzzy prenatal body _____, which drops off within a few days after birth.
5. **vernix caseosa:** Oily substance on a neonate's skin that protects against _____.
6. _____: Lack of oxygen, which may cause brain damage.
7. _____: Fetal waste matter, excreted during the first few days after birth.
8. **neonatal jaundice:** Condition, in many newborn babies, caused by immaturity of _____ and evidenced by yellowish appearance; can cause brain damage if not treated promptly.

### LEARNING OBJECTIVES FOR SECTION III

After reading and reviewing this section of Chapter 5, you should be able to do the following.

1. Describe the typical size and appearance of a newborn and identify several distinctive features that change during the neonatal period.

**Section IV   Is the Baby Healthy?**

## FRAMEWORK FOR SECTION IV

A.      Medical and Behavioral Screening
     1.   The Apgar Scale

     2.   Assessing Neurological Status: Brazelton Scale

     3.   Neonatal Screening for Medical Conditions

B.      Complications of Childbirth
     1.   Low Birthweight

     2.   Postmaturity

     3.   Stillborn

C.      Can A Supportive Environment Overcome Effects of Birth Complications?
     1.   The Infant Health and Development Studies

     2.   The Kaual Study

## IMPORTANT TERMS FOR SECTION IV

**Completion:**  Fill in the blanks to complete the definitions of key terms for this section of Chapter 5.

1.   **birth** _____ : Injury sustained at the time of birth due to oxygen deprivation, mechanical injury, infection, or disease.
2.   **low birthweight:** Weight of less than _____ pounds at birth because of prematurity or being small for date.
3.   **preterm (premature) infants:** Infants born before completing the _____ week of gestation.
4.   **small-for-date (small-for-gestational age) infants:** Infants whose birthweight is less than that of _____ percent of babies of the same gestational age, as a result of slow fetal growth.
5.   _____ : Referring to a fetus not yet born as of 2 weeks after the due date or 42 weeks after the mother's last menstrual period.
6.   **electronic fetal monitoring:** Mechanical monitoring of fetal _____ during labor and delivery.
7.   _____ **scale:** Standard measurement of a newborn's condition; it assesses appearance, pulse, grimace, activity, and respiration.
8.   _____ **Neonatal Behavioral Assessment Scale:** Neurological and behavioral test to measure neonates' response to the environment; it assesses interactive behaviors, motor behaviors, physiological control, and response to stress.

## LEARNING OBJECTIVES FOR SECTION IV

After reading and reviewing this section of Chapter 5, you should be able to do the following.

1.   Explain the difference between preterm (premature) and small-for-date infants and between low birthweight and very low birthweight.

2. Name four types of factors that put women at risk of bearing low-birthweight babies, and give an example of each type.

3. Compare low-birthweight rates in the United States with those in other countries and cite possible reasons for the high rates among African-Americans.

4. Identify consequences of low birthweight.

5. Describe methods of care and treatment of low-birthweight babies that can improve their chances of survival.

6. Discuss the role of environmental factors in the long-term outlook for children with low birthweight or other birth complications.

7. Identify considerations involved, when a baby is postmature, in deciding whether to induce labor or deliver by the cesarean method.

8. Describe the typical process of grieving for a stillborn baby.

9. State reasons for using electronic fetal monitoring during childbirth and drawbacks of its use.

10. Identify and describe three tests given to neonates to assess their health or the normality of their responses or to identify babies with specific correctable defects.

## Section V   Newborns and Their Parents

FRAMEWORK FOR SECTION V

A.      Childbirth and Bonding
B.      Getting to Know the Baby: States of Arousal and Activity Levels
C.      How Parenthood Affects a Marriage

## IMPORTANT TERMS FOR SECTION V

**Completion:**  Fill in the blanks to complete the definitions of key terms for this section of Chapter 5.
   1. **imprinting:** Instinctive form of learning in which, during a _____ period in early development, a young animal forms an attachment to the first moving object it sees, usually the mother.
   2. **mother-infant** _____: Mother's feeling of close, caring connection with her newborn.
   3. state of _____: An infant's degree of alertness; his or her condition, at a given moment, in the periodic daily cycle of wakefulness, sleep, and activity.

## LEARNING OBJECTIVES FOR SECTION V

After reading and reviewing this section of Chapter 5, you should be able to do the following.
   1. Distinguish between the processes of bonding after birth that affect animal and human babies.

2. Describe typical patterns of eating, sleeping, and waking in neonates, tell how they change during infancy, and explain the developmental significance of variations in these early patterns.

3. Suggest several methods of comforting a crying baby.

4. Identify two common patterns of change in marital relationships after the birth of a baby, and compare the adjustment of adoptive parents with that of biological parents.

# CHAPTER 5 QUIZ

**Matching--Numbers:** For each of the items in the column at the left, fill in the correct number from the column at the right.

1. Number of weeks in the neonatal period
   _____

   a.  1

2. Age below which a woman is at risk of bearing an underweight infant _____

   b.  4

3. Age above which a woman is at risk of bearing an underweight infant _____

   c.  6

4. Number of weeks after the last menstrual period at which a birth is considered postmature _____

   d.  7

   e.  16

5. Approximate length in inches of the average newborn _____

   f.  17

6. Number of minutes after delivery when Apgar scale is first administered _____

   g.  20

7. Minimum score attained by about 99 percent of infants on second administration of Apgar scale
   _____

   h.  35

8. Average number of hours per day a newborn sleeps _____

   i.  40

9. Percentage of expectant mothers in the United States attended by midwives in 1995
   _____

   j.  42

10. Percentage of Dutch babies born at home
    _____

**Multiple-Choice**: Circle the choice that best completes or answers each item.

1. The birth process is set in motion by
   a. the mother's uterus
   b. the mother's cervix
   c. the fetus's brain
   d. none of the above; the process is automatic

2. During the first stage of labor
   a. the mother's cervix dilates to permit passage of the baby's head out of the uterus
   b. the mother experiences "false" labor pains
   c. the mother bears down to permit passage of the baby
   d. the baby's head begins to move through the cervix and vaginal canal

3. For a woman having her first baby, the movement of the baby through the cervix and vaginal canal generally takes approximately
   a. 10 minutes
   b. 30 minutes
   c. 1½ hours
   d. 12 hours

4. The umbilical cord and placenta are expelled from the womb during which stage of labor?
   a. first
   b. second
   c. third
   d. fourth

5. Research has established that medicated delivery
   a. causes permanent deficits in motor and physiological response
   b. causes mothers to feel more positive toward their babies
   c. has no effect on babies
   d. none of the above; studies have yielded contradictory results

6. Natural childbirth involves educating and training women in order to eliminate
   a. severe contractions
   b. fear and pain
   c. the need for medical monitoring
   d. the need for attending physicians

7. Which of the following is not an element of the Lamaze method of childbirth?
   a. education about childbirth
   b. control of breathing
   c. coaching
   d. concentration on birth contractions

8. Which of the following statements about cesarean delivery is true?
   a. The rate of cesarean deliveries in the United States increased during the 1990s.
   b. Cesarean deliveries are more often performed on younger mothers.
   c. Cesarean deliveries are more often performed during first births.
   d. Risk of infection is lower with cesarean delivery than with vaginal delivery.

9. In comparison with women attended by physicians, women using nurse-midwives for low-risk hospital births tend to have
   a. more anesthesia
   b. fewer episiotomies
   c. poorer outcomes
   d. induced labor

10. A doula is
    a. another term for midwife
    b. an experienced companion who provides emotional support during childbirth
    c. needed chiefly during forceps deliveries
    d. called upon to administer anesthesia

11. The weight of an average newborn is about
    a. 5 pounds
    b. 6½ pounds
    c. 7½ pounds
    d. 9 pounds

12. A newborn baby's head is about what proportion of its body length?
    a. one-eighth
    b. one-fourth
    c. one-third
    d. one-half

13. The umbilical cord is essential to all but which of the following fetal body systems?
    a. circulatory
    b. respiratory
    c. gastrointestinal
    d. temperature regulation

14. The brain grows from about what percent of its adult weight at birth to about what percent of its adult weight at 1 year?
    a. 1 to 10
    b. 10 to 50
    c. 25 to 70
    d. 50 to 100

15. At birth, the cells in the brain
    a. number fewer than half the quantity present in adulthood
    b. are fully connected but not yet differentiated by function
    c. consist only of nuclei
    d. are most fully developed in the structures below the cortex
16. All but which of the following are reflex behaviors?
    a. coughing
    b. crawling
    c. shivering
    d. yawning
17. Low-birthweight babies are defined as those weighing less than
    a. 3 pounds
    b. 4½ pounds
    c. 5½ pounds
    d. 7 pounds
18. Other things being equal, which of the following women would be least likely to deliver a low-birthweight baby?
    a. 30-year-old bearing her second child 2 years after the birth of the first
    b. 23-year old smoker bearing her first child
    c. 35-year-old bearing twins
    d. 28-year-old who was herself low-birthweight
19. Which of the following women is most likely to deliver a low-birthweight baby?
    a. Asian American
    b. Hispanic American
    c. African American
    d. white American
20. Which of the following is not a common problem among low-birthweight babies?
    a. high body temperature
    b. irregular breathing
    c. infection
    d. weak sucking
21. Very low-birthweight babies who later have problems in school tend to be
    a. female
    b. premature
    c. small for gestational age
    d. twins
22. Studies have found all but which of the following factors important in helping low-birthweight children overcome their early disadvantages?
    a. socioeconomic status
    b. number of siblings
    c. quality of the caregiving environment
    d. duration of the intervention
23. Postmature babies tend to be
    a. long and thin
    b. long and fat
    c. short and thin
    d. short and fat
24. "False positive" readings on electronic fetal monitors during childbirth suggest that fetuses
    a. lack oxygen when in fact they do not
    b. have normal heartbeats when in fact they do not
    c. are at risk of premature expulsion when in fact they are not
    d. are in position for delivery when in fact they are not
25. Which of the following is not assessed by the Brazelton Neonatal Behavioral Assessment Scale?
    a. alertness
    b. respiration
    c. muscle tone
    d. respiration and muscle tone
26. Imprinting seems to result from
    a. a predisposition toward learning during a critical period
    b. placing an infant in the "strange situation"
    c. an adult's directing and organizing a child's learning
    d. a child's mental manipulation of incoming sensory information
27. Research on mother-infant bonding has established that babies who are separated from their mothers immediately after birth are more likely to
    a. die in infancy
    b. show cognitive deficits
    c. have difficulty bonding with the mother
    d. none of the above

28. Which of the following sleep patterns is typical of neonates?
    a. six to eight sleep periods of 2 to 3 hours each
    b. four or five sleep periods of approximately 4 hours each
    c. shorter sleep periods in the daytime and longer sleep periods at night
    d. none of the above; sleep patterns are so individual that no typical pattern can be described

29. Which of the following neonatal behaviors seems to be an indicator of temperament?
    a. amount of crying
    b. amount of sleeping
    c. both a and b
    d. neither a nor b

**True or False?** In the blank following each item, write T (for true) or F (for false). In the space below each item, if the statement is false, rewrite it to make it true.

1. The first stage of labor for a first baby typically lasts 12 hours or more. _____

2. The first stage of labor is often painful because of the stretching of the vagina as the baby's head pushes against it. _____

3. The mother has no control over the baby's progress through the vaginal canal. _____

4. In most childbirths, general anesthesia is routinely administered to the mother. _____

5. In the Lamaze method, an expectant mother is conditioned to relax her muscles in response to the voice of her partner or another labor "coach." _____

6. The rate of cesarean deliveries in the United States is nearly four times as high as in 1970. _____

7. The struggle involved in vaginal birth apparently triggers the release of stress hormones that help babies survive and adjust to life outside the womb. _____

8. It is safer for a woman who has had a cesarean delivery to have vaginal delivery in subsequent births. _____

9. In the United States, 99 percent of babies are born in hospitals. _____

10. Newborns lose weight during the first few days of life. _____

11. A newborn who has thin skin, hair covering the body, and swollen breasts with secretions is probably unhealthy. _____

12. About half of all babies develop neonatal jaundice a few days after birth. _____

# ANSWER KEY FOR CHAPTER 5

## CHAPTER 5 REVIEW

### Important Terms for Section I and Section II

1. natural
2. prepared
3. cesarean
4. humanize

### Important Terms for Section III

1. neonate
2. neonatal
3. head
4. hair
5. infection
6. anoxia
7. meconium
8. liver

### Important Terms for Section IV

1. trauma
2. 5½
3. thirty-seventh
4. 90
5. postmature
6. heartbeat
7. Apgar
8. Brazelton

### Important Terms for Section V

1. critical
2. bond
3. arousal

## CHAPTER 5 QUIZ

### Matching--Numbers

1. b
2. f
3. i
4. j
5. g
6. a
7. d
8. e
9. c
10. h

### Multiple-Choice

1. a
2. a
3. c
4. c
5. d
6. b
7. d
8. c
9. b
10. b
11. c
12. b
13. d
14. c
15. d
16. b
17. c
18. a
19. c
20. a
21. c
22. b
23. a
24. a
25. b
26. a
27. d
28. a
29. b

### True or False?

1. T
2. F-The first stage of labor is often painful primarily because of the stretching, or dilation, of the cervix.
3. F-The mother's bearing down with her abdominal muscles during each contraction helps the baby leave her body.
4. F-General anesthesia is rarely used today.
5. T
6. T
7. T
8. F-An attempted vaginal delivery following an initial cesarean delivery may carry greater risk of major complications, especially if labor is unsuccessful and a cesarean delivery must be done after all.

9. T
10. T
11. F-Thin skin, body hair, and swollen breasts with secretions are normal attributes of many newborns.
12. T

# CHAPTER 6
# PHYSICAL DEVELOPMENT AND HEALTH DURING THE FIRST THREE YEARS

## OVERVIEW

Chapter 6 describes babies' physical growth and their rapidly developing sensory capabilities and motor skills, as well as threats to life and health. In this chapter, the authors:

❑ Describe the growth of body and brain and explain how this growth may be affected by environmental influences

❑ Discuss how babies should be nourished

❑ Trace highlights of infants' sensory and motor development and discuss maturational and contextual influences on motor development

❑ Discuss factors that contribute to infant mortality and possible causes and prevention of Sudden Infant Death Syndrome (SIDS)

❑ Report on trends in immunization against childhood diseases

## GUIDEPOSTS FOR STUDY

6.1 How do babies grow and what influences their growth?

6.2 How and what should infants be fed?

6.3 How does the brain develop and how do environmental factors affect its early growth?

6.4 How do the senses develop during infancy?

6.5 What are some early milestones in motor development?

6.6 What are some influences on motor development?

6.7 How can we enhance babies' chances of survival and health?

## CHAPTER 6 REVIEW

**Section I  Growth and Nutrition**

FRAMEWORK FOR SECTION I

A.      Patterns of Growth

B.      Influences on Growth

C.      Nourishment

LEARNING OBJECTIVES FOR SECTION I

After reading and reviewing this section of Chapter 6, you should be able to do the following.

 1. Describe typical changes in weight, height, body shape, and tooth development during the first 3 years.

2. Give two examples of the cephalocaudal principle of physical development and two examples of the proximodistal principle.

3. Discuss genetic and environmental influences on body growth.

4. Explain the importance of nutrition and the health advantages of breastfeeding.

5. Discuss the incidence of breastfeeding among demographic groups and ways to encourage breastfeeding.

6. Tell at what ages it is advisable to introduce cow's milk, fruit juices, and solid foods.

7. Summarize research on the long-term effects of obesity in infancy.

**Section II The Brain and Reflex Behavior**

## FRAMEWORK FOR SECTION II

A.  Building the Brain

    1.  Major Parts of the Brain

    2.  Brain cells

    3.  Myelination

B.  Early Reflexes

C.  Molding the Brain: The Role of Experience

## IMPORTANT TERMS FOR SECTION II

**Completion:** Fill in the blanks to complete the definition of the key term for this section of Chapter 6.

1.  **plasticity:** modifiability, or "molding," of the brain through early _____.

2.  **central nervous system:**_____ and spinal cord.

3.  **neurons**:_____ cells.

4.  **myelination:** Process of coating neurons with a fatty substance that enables faster _____ between cells.

## LEARNING OBJECTIVES FOR SECTION II

After reading and reviewing this section of Chapter 6, you should be able to do the following.

1.  Describe the growth and development of the central nervous system before and after birth.

2.  Name at least four primitive reflexes; explain their purpose and the significance of their disappearance during infancy, and give an example of ethnic or cultural variations in reflex behavior.

3.  Explain how an infant's brain is "molded" by experience.

4. Describe animal studies that support the idea of plasticity of the brain, and give evidence of the effect of environmental deprivation in humans.

## Section III  Early Sensory Capacities

### FRAMEWORK FOR SECTION III

A.      Touch and Pain

B.      Smell and Taste

C.      Hearing

D.      Sight

### IMPORTANT TERM FOR SECTION III

**Completion:** Fill in the blanks to complete the definition of the key term for this section of Chapter 6.

1. **visual** _____: An infant's tendency to look longer at certain stimuli than at others, which depends on the ability to make visual distinctions.

### LEARNING OBJECTIVES FOR SECTION III

After reading and reviewing this section of Chapter 6, you should be able to do the following.

1. Summarize research on the capacities of the five senses at birth and in the early weeks and months thereafter.

2. Discuss the need for, and effectiveness of, anesthesia in circumcision and other surgical procedures done on infants.

3. Trace the early development of color perception, focus, and binocular vision.

4. Explain the significance of very young babies' visual preferences.

5. Tell how the origins of the senses of smell and taste differ.

6. Explain the adaptive value of newborns' "sweet tooth" and discuss the effectiveness of sweet tastes in calming neonates?

7. Give evidence that hearing develops in the womb.

**Section IV Motor Development**

FRAMEWORK FOR SECTION IV

A.  Milestones of Motor Development
   1.  Head Control
   2.  Hand Control
   3.  Locomotion

B.  How Motor Development Occurs: Maturation in Context
C.  Motor Development and Perception
D.  Cultural Influences on Motor Development
E.  Training Motor Skills Experimentally

## IMPORTANT TERMS FOR SECTION IV

**Completion:** Fill in the blank to complete the definitions of key terms for this section of Chapter 6.

1. **systems of** _____: Increasingly complex combinations of simpler, previously acquired skills, which permit a wider or more precise range of movement and more control of the environment.

2. _____ _____**Screening Test:** Screening test given to children 1 month to 6 years old to determine whether they are developing normally; it assesses gross motor skills, fine motor skills, language development, and personality and social development.

3. **visual** _____: Apparatus designed to give an illusion of depth and used to assess depth perception in infants.

4. **depth perception:** Ability to perceive objects and surfaces _____-dimensionally.


## LEARNING OBJECTIVES FOR SECTION IV

After reading and reviewing this section of Chapter 6, you should be able to do the following.

1. Identify three maturational principles that affect motor development, and tell how they affect the development of the precision grip and the ability to walk.

2. Discuss Esther Thelen's critique of traditional maturational theory and her alternative explanation for early motor development.

3. Describe the Denver Developmental Screening Test and explain what is meant by an "average" baby.

4. List at least five milestones of motor development in infancy and toddlerhood and the average age at which each is attained.

5. Explain the significance of crawling for physical, cognitive, and emotional development.

6. Tell how motor development influences depth perception and haptic perception.

7. Give examples of differing rates of development of motor skills in different societies or cultures and suggest reasons for these differences.

8. Discuss findings on whether early training can speed up motor development.

**Section V  Health**

FRAMEWORK FOR SECTION V

A.   Reducing Infant Mortality
  1.   Trends in Infant Mortality
  2.   Sudden Infant Death Syndrome
  3.   Death from Injuries

B.   Immunization for Better Health

IMPORTANT TERMS FOR SECTION V

**Completion:** Fill in the blanks to complete the definitions of key terms for this section of Chapter 6.
  1. **infant mortality rate:** Proportion of babies born alive who die within the first _____.
  2. sudden infant death syndrome (SIDS): Sudden and unexpected death of an apparently
        _____ infant.

## LEARNING OBJECTIVES FOR SECTION V

After reading and reviewing this section of Chapter 6, you should be able to do the following.

1. Give reasons why infant mortality has been declining.

2. Compare the infant mortality rate in the United States with rates in other industrialized nations.

3. Explain the relationship between infant mortality and low birthweight, and analyze differences in infant mortality among ethnic groups.

4. Cite possible explanations and risk factors for sudden infant death syndrome (SIDS) and recommendations for prevention.

5. Summarize trends in immunization rates for preventable childhood illnesses, and explain why some parents hesitate to immunize their children.

6. Describe cultural differences in sleeping arrangements for infants.

# CHAPTER 6 QUIZ

**Matching--Numbers:** Match each description in the left-hand column with the correct number in the right-hand column.

1. Percent by which the weight of a 1-year-old baby's brain compares with its full adult weight _____

2. Age in months at which the average baby's birthweight doubles _____

3. Number of teeth the average child has by 2½ years _____

4. Height in inches of the typical 1-year-old _____

5. Age in months at which the average baby can build a tower of two cubes _____

6. Minimum number of months for which breastfeeding is recommended _____

7. Age in months at which infants can distinguish such speech sounds as "ba" and "pa" _____

8. Age in months by which the average baby can walk up steps _____

9. Age in months by which almost all infants can keep heads erect while being supported in a sitting position _____

10. Percentage by which SIDS cases in the United States have decreased since 1979 _____

11. Percentage of U.S. 19- to 35-month-olds fully immunized in 1995 _____

a.  1

b.  4

c.  5

d.  12

e.  15

f.  17

g.  20

h.  30

i.  40

j.  70

k.  75

**Multiple-Choice:** Circle the choice that best completes or answers each item.

1. According to the cephalocaudal and proximodistal principles, it would take longest for a baby to develop the ability to
   a. focus the eyes
   b. wiggle the toes
   c. hold a rattle
   d. kick the legs

2. Body growth is fastest in which of these periods?
   a. birth to 1 year
   b. 1 year to 2 years
   c. 2 years to 3 years
   d. 13 years to 15 years

3. All but which of the following are considered benefits of breastfeeding over bottle-feeding for newborns?
   a. contains less fat
   b. less allergenic
   c. protects against infections
   d. is more digestible

4. Myelination
   a. is a process for making formula as much like breast milk as possible.
   b. is the multiplication of connections in the brain during the early months of life.
   c. coats nerve pathways to facilitate neural communication
   d. is another term for plasticity.

5. Studies of Romanian orphans suggest that extreme environmental deprivation
   a. Can permanently stunt the growth of a child's brain.
   b. Can lead to neurological abnormalities and developmental delays, but these may be overcome by an improved environment.
   c. Has no effect on brain growth, which is controlled by maturation.
   d. none of the above; studies of environmental effects on the human brain cannot be done for ethical reasons.

6. It appears that the first sense to develop is
   a. sight
   b. hearing
   c. touch
   d. taste

7. An infant's vision typically becomes 20/20 by about the
   a. third day
   b. fourth week
   c. third month
   d. sixth month

8. The ability of newborns to differentiate between patterns is predictive of their
   a. intelligence
   b. artistic talent
   c. visual acuity
   d. independence

9. Which of the following tastes would most newborns prefer?
   a. pure water
   b. sugar solution
   c. lemon juice
   d. none of the above; newborns cannot discriminate among these tastes

10. All but which of the following statements about infants' hearing are true?
   a. Newborns show signs of having heard sounds in the womb.
   b. Hearing improves immediately after birth.
   c. A 3-day-old baby can distinguish the mother's voice from a stranger's.
   d. Auditory discrimination at 4 months predicts IQ at 5 years.

11. All but which of the following are present in newborns?
   a. precision grip
   b. directional smell
   c. visual preference
   d. auditory discrimination

12. According to Esther Thelen, early motor development
   a. is largely automatic
   b. is controlled by the brain's maturation
   c. reflects a shift from subcortical to cortical activity
   d. results from problem solving in a physical and social context

13. A child's failure to pass an item on the Denver Developmental Screening Test is considered a sign of developmental delay if what percent of children the same age ordinarily pass it?
   a. 50
   b. 75
   c. 80
   d. 90

14. The average baby begins to roll over purposely at about
   a. 3 weeks
   b. 2 months
   c. 3 months
   d. 5 months

15. Crawling helps to promote "social referencing," meaning that a crawling baby is more likely than one who does not yet crawl to
   a. interact with other babies
   b. perceive how near or far away a person or object is
   c. compare his or her size with that of adults
   d. look at the mother to check whether a situation is safe

16. Depth perception may be aided by all but which of the following?
   a. kinetic cues
   b. binocular cues
   c. pattern vision
   d. haptic perception

17. Which of the following is likely to walk earliest?
   a. African baby
   b. Asian baby
   c. American baby
   d. Mexican baby

18. According to research, which of the following statements about the environment and motor development is true?
   a. Because many aspects of motor development are genetically programmed, the environment cannot retard it.
   b. Training 2-month-olds in "stepping" can lead to earlier walking.
   c. Early training in one ability carries over to other abilities.
   d. Infant "walkers" have helped many children to walk early.

19. The infant mortality rate in the United States is lower
    a. than ever before
    b. among black babies than among white babies
    c. than in any other industrialized nation
    d. than the rate in Singapore
20. More than two-thirds of infant deaths occur within how long after birth?
    a. 10 hours
    b. 4 weeks
    c. 3 months
    d. 1 year
21. Research suggests that one causal factor in sudden infant death syndrome may be
    a. choking
    b. vomiting
    c. contagious infection
    d. parental smoking
22. An infant sharing the "family bed" is likely to be all but which of the following?
    a. African American
    b. fed more promptly
    c. demanding of attention
    d. vulnerable to sudden infant death syndrome
23. Which of the following statements about immunization is true?
    a. The incidence of vaccine-preventable illnesses has increased during the 1990s.
    b. Immunization rates are lower among poor and some minority families.
    c. Certain vaccines are likely to cause brain damage.
    d. Vaccines are effective only in children.

**True or False?** In the blank following each item, write T (for true) or F (for false). In the space below each item, if the statement is false, rewrite it to make it true.

1. By the second birthday, the average child weighs 4 times as much as at birth. _____

2. Most babies get the first tooth at about 3 to 4 months. _____

3. Normal physical development seems to follow a consistent sequence. _____

4. Most newborn babies in the United States are bottle-fed. _____

5. Breastfeeding is most popular among poor and African American women. _____

6. AIDS can be transmitted to a breastfeeding baby through the mother's milk. _____

7. Pediatric nutritionists recommend starting solid foods by 2 months to foster healthy growth and help babies sleep through the night. _____

8. Babies should be given skim milk to keep them from getting too fat. _____

9. A fat baby or toddler is more likely than a thin one to become a fat adult. _____

10. Chronic undernourishment, before or after birth, can result in brain damage. _____

11. A mother's depression can affect her infant's brain activity. _____

12. Studies of Romanian orphans show that the effects of early sensory deprivation on an infant's brain are irreversible. _____

13. Circumcision is painless for an 8-day-old baby, because nerve endings are not yet developed. _____

14. Newborn babies can distinguish among primary colors. _____

15. Newborns prefer complex patterns to simple ones. _____

16. Infants recognize the smell of their mothers from birth. _____

17. Esther Thelen's work suggests that infants might be able to walk sooner if their legs could support their weight. _____

18. According to Thelen, a baby who never saw anyone walk would be unlikely to learn how to walk. _____

19. The Denver norms are valid for children worldwide. _____

20. On average, babies learn to walk well a few weeks after they learn to stand alone. _____

21. Babies at 2 to 3 months can perceive heights but do not fear them. _____

22. Early perceptual abilities are limited by an infant's level of motor development. _____

23. Babies in all cultures develop basic motor skills at about the same rates. _____

24. Black babies are more than twice as likely as white babies to die within the first year. _____

25. Sudden infant death syndrome can be prevented by putting a baby down to sleep on the stomach. _____

26. More than nine out of ten 5-year-olds have had all their required immunizations. _____

# ANSWER KEY FOR CHAPTER 6

## CHAPTER 6 REVIEW

### Important Terms for Section II
1. experience
2. brain
3. nerve
4. communication

### Important Term for Section III
1. preference

### Important Terms for Section IV
1. action
2. Denver Developmental
3. cliff
4. three

### Important Terms for Section V
1. year
2. healthy

## CHAPTER 6 QUIZ

### Matching--Numbers
1. j
2. c
3. g
4. h
5. e
6. d
7. a
8. f
9. b
10. i
11. k

### Multiple-Choice
1. b
2. a
3. a
4. c
5. b
6. c
7. d
8. a
9. b
10. b
11. a
12. d
13. d
14. c
15. d
16. c
17. a
18. b
19. a
20. b
21. d
22. c
23. b

### True or False?
1. T
2. F-Most babies get the first tooth between 5 and 9 months.
3. T
4. F-Nearly 60 percent of newborns are breastfed.
5. F-Poor and African American women are least likely to breastfeed.
6. T
7. F-Pediatric nutritionists recommend withholding solid foods until the second half of the first year.
8. F-Babies need the calories in whole milk.
9. F-Any correlation between obesity in infancy and adulthood is related to obesity in the family.
10. T
11. T
12. F-Studies of Romanian orphans suggest that proper environmental stimulation can overcome effects of early environmental deprivation.
13. F-Even on the first day of life, babies can feel pain, and babies show signs of pain when circumcision is performed without anesthesia.
14. F-Infants cannot distinguish among primary colors until 2 to 4 months.
15. T
16. F-Infants learn to recognize their mother's smell within the first few days after birth.
17. T
18. F-According to Thelen, all normal babies develop basic motor skills such as walking because they are built approximately alike and have similar challenges and needs.
19. F-The Denver norms were standardized on a western population and may not be valid for children in nonwestern societies.
20. T
21. T

22. T
23. F-Babies in various cultures have been found to develop basic motor skills at different rates.
24. T in the U.S.
25. F-Sudden infant death syndrome can be prevented by putting a baby down to sleep on the back or side.
26. T

# CHAPTER 7
# COGNITIVE DEVELOPMENT
# DURING THE FIRST THREE YEARS

## OVERVIEW

Chapter 7 examines the rapid cognitive development that takes place during the first 3 years of life. In this chapter, the authors:

❑ Compare the behaviorist, psychometric, Piagetian, information-processing, cognitive neuroscience, and social-contextual approaches to understanding cognitive development

❑ Describe research on infants' learning and memory, and their development of concepts about the physical world

❑ Consider ways to assess infants' and toddlers' intelligence

❑ Outline stages in language development during the first 3 years; compare theories about language development; and discuss influences on language development and preparation for reading.

❑ Present findings on the growth of competence and how parents and other adults can foster it

## GUIDEPOSTS FOR STUDY

7.1 How do infants learn and how long can they remember?

7.2 Can infants' and toddlers' intelligence be measured and how can it be improved?

7.3 How did Piaget describe infants' and toddlers' cognitive development and how have his claims stood up under later scrutiny?

7.4 How can we measure infants' ability to process information and how does this ability relate to future intelligence?

7.5 When do babies begin to think about characteristics of the physical world?

7.6 What can brain research reveal about the development of cognitive skills?

7.7 How does social interaction with adults advance cognitive competence?

7.8 How do babies develop language?

7.9 What influences contribute to linguistic progress?

## CHAPTER 7 REVIEW

**Section I  Studying Cognitive Development: Classic Approaches**

FRAMEWORK FOR SECTION I

A.     Behaviorist Approach: Basic Mechanics of Learning
    1.   Classical and Operant Conditioning
    2.   Infant Memory

B.     Psychometric Approach: Developmental and Intelligence Testing
    1.   Testing Infants and Toddlers
    2.   Socioeconomic Status, Parenting Practices, and IQ

3. Assessing the Impact of the Home Environment
4. Early Intervention

C. Piagetian Approach: The Sensorimotor Stage
1. Sensorimotor Stage
2. Development of Knowledge about Objects and Space
3. What Abilities May Develop Earlier than Piaget Thought

## IMPORTANT TERMS FOR SECTION I

**Completion:** Fill in the blanks to complete the definitions of key terms for this section of Chapter 7.

1. _____ **behavior:** Behavior that is goal-oriented (conscious and deliberate) and adaptive to circumstances and conditions of life.

2. _____ **approach:** Approach to the study of cognitive development based on learning theory, which is concerned with the basic mechanics of learning.

3. _____ **approach:** Approach to the study of cognitive development that seeks to measure the quantity of intelligence a person possesses.

4. _____ **approach:** Approach to the study of cognitive development based on _____'s theory, which describes qualitative stages, or typical changes, in children's and adolescents' cognitive functioning.

5. _____ **conditioning:** Kind of learning in which a previously neutral stimulus (one that does not originally elicit a particular response) acquires the power to elicit the response after the stimulus is repeatedly associated with another stimulus that ordinarily does elicit the response.

6. _____ **conditioning:** Form of learning in which a person tends to repeat a behavior that has been reinforced or to cease a behavior that has been punished.

7. **IQ (intelligence _____) tests:** Psychometric tests that seek to measure how much intelligence a person has by comparing her or his performance with standardized norms.

8. **standardized norms:** Standards for evaluating performance of persons who take an intelligence test, obtained from scores of a large, _____ sample who took the test while it was in preparation.

9. _____ **Scales of Infant Development:** Standardized test of infants' mental and motor development.

10. **Home Observation for Measurement of the Environment (HOME):** Instrument to measure the influence of the home environment on children's _____ growth.

11. **developmental _____ _____:** Aspects of the home environment that seem to be necessary for normal cognitive and psychosocial development to occur.

12. **early _____:** Systematic process of planning and providing therapeutic and educational services to families that need help in meeting infants', toddlers', or preschool children's developmental needs.

13. **sensorimotor stage:** In Piaget's theory, the first stage in cognitive development, during which infants (from birth to approximately _____ year[s]) learn through their developing senses and motor activity.

14. **schemes:** In Piaget's terminology, basic cognitive _____ consisting of organized patterns of behavior used in different kinds of situations.

15. **circular _____:** In Piaget's terminology, processes by which an infant learns to reproduce desired occurrences originally discovered by chance.

16. **representational ability:** In Piaget's terminology, capacity to mentally represent objects and experiences, largely through the use of _____.

17. _____ **imitation:** In Piaget's terminology, reproduction of an observed behavior after the passage of time by calling up a stored symbol of it.

18. **pretend play:** Play involving _____ people or situations; also called fantasy play, dramatic play, or imaginative play.

19. **object permanence:** In Piaget's terminology, the understanding that a person or object still exists when out of _____.

20. _____ **imitation:** Imitation with parts of one's body that one cannot see (e.g., the mouth).
21. _____ **imitation:** Imitation with parts of one's body that one can see (e.g., the hands and the feet).

## LEARNING OBJECTIVES FOR SECTION I

After reading and reviewing this section of Chapter 7, you should be able to do the following.

1. Compare the concerns and methods of the behaviorist, psychometric, and Piagetian approaches to understanding and assessing cognitive development.

2. Describe how classical and operant conditioning work and give an example of how each can be studied in infants.

3. Summarize what experiments using operant conditioning have found out about infants' memory capabilities.

4. Explain why and how intelligence tests are standardized, and the importance of validity and reliability.

5. Explain why it is difficult to measure infants' and toddlers' intelligence reliably.

6. State a purpose for administering developmental tests to infants and describe one such test.

7. Describe an instrument used to measure the impact of the home environment on cognitive growth, and name at least two factors that seem to affect infants' and toddlers' future intelligence test scores.

8. Identify six developmental priming mechanisms that help children get ready for schooling.

9. List at least six suggestions for fostering infants' and toddlers' cognitive and social competence.

10. Describe an early educational intervention for disadvantaged children, and identify five factors in the effectiveness of such a program.

11. Identify the major changes that occur during the sensorimotor stage, according to Piaget.

12. List the substages of Piaget's sensorimotor stage, describe the development that occurs during each substage, and give an example of typical behavior at each substage.

13. Explain how representational ability makes possible deferred imitation and pretend play.

14. Trace the development of object permanence through the six substages of Piaget's sensorimotor stage, and point out how such changes can be seen in the game of peekaboo.

15. Assess research on the ages at which invisible imitation and deferred imitation begin.

16. Explain why studies using elicited imitation have found infants capable of long-term recall at an earlier age than Piaget believed possible.

**Section II Studying Cognitive Development: Newer Approaches**

## FRAMEWORK FOR SECTION II

A.  Information-Processing Approach: Perceptions and Representations
    1.  Habituation
    2.  Early Perceptual and Processing Abilities
    3.  Information Processing as a Predictor of Intelligence
    4.  Violation of Expectations and the Development of Thought

B.  Cognitive Neuroscience Approach: The Brain's Cognitive Structures
C.  Social-Contextual Approach: Learning from Interactions with Caregivers

## IMPORTANT TERMS FOR SECTION II

**Completion:** Fill in the blanks to complete the definitions of key terms for this section of Chapter 7.

1.  **information-processing approach:** Approach to the study of cognitive development by observing and analyzing the mental processes involved in _____ and handling information.
2.  **cognitive neuroscience approach:** Approach to the study of cognitive development by examining brain structures and measuring neurological _____.
3.  **social-_____ approach:** Approach to the study of cognitive development by focusing on the influence of environmental aspects of the learning process, particularly parents and other caregivers.
4.  **habituation:** Simple type of learning in which _____ with a stimulus reduces, slows, or stops a response. Compare dishabituation.
5.  **dishabituation:** Increase in _____ after presentation of a new stimulus. Compare habituation.
6.  **visual-recognition memory:** Ability to distinguish a familiar visual _____ from an unfamiliar one.
7.  **visual _____ preference:** Infant's preference for new rather than familiar sights.
8.  **cross-modal _____:** Ability to identify by sight an item earlier felt but not seen.
9.  **exploratory _____:** Cognitive capacity underlying the variance in toddlers' ability to sustain attention and engage in sophisticated symbolic play.
10. **violation of expectations:** Research method in which an infant's tendency to dishabituate to a stimulus that conflicts with previous experience is taken as evidence that the infant recognizes the new stimulus as _____.
11. **causality:** Awareness that one event causes _____.
12. _____ **memory:** Memory, generally of facts, names, and events, which is intentional and conscious. Compare _____ memory.
13. _____ **memory:** Memory, generally of habits and skills, which does not require conscious recall; sometimes called procedural memory. Compare _____ memory.
14. **working memory:** _____-term storage of information being actively processed.
15. _____ **participation:** In Vygotsky's terminology, participation of an adult in a child's activity in a manner that helps to structure the activity and to bring the child's understanding of it closer to the understanding of the adult.

## LEARNING OBJECTIVES FOR SECTION II

After reading and reviewing this section of Chapter 7, you should be able to do the following.

1.  Compare the concerns and methods of the information-processing, cognitive neuroscience, and social-contextual approaches to understanding and assessing cognitive development.

2. Name and describe four information-processing abilities that seem to be predictors of childhood intelligence.

3. Explain how the violation-of-expectations method can be used to test the age at which babies acquire the capacity to reason about the physical world, and name three abilities which, according to this research, may be achieved earlier than Piaget thought.

4. Trace developmental changes in infants' ways of thinking about physical phenomena.

5. Give evidence that a responsive caregiver can enhance a baby's ability to process information.

6. Distinguish between implicit memory and explicit memory, identify the brain structures that seem to be involved in each, and explain how preexplicit memory evolves into explicit memory.

7. Tell what working memory does, and explain its relationship to the development of object permanence.

8. Compare Vygotsky's concepts of guided participation and scaffolding, and explain why guided participation may be a more useful way of describing early cognitive development in some cultures.

**Section III  Language Development**

FRAMEWORK FOR SECTION III

A.       Sequence of Early Language Development
  1.   Early Vocalization
  2.   Recognizing Language Sounds
  3.   Gestures
  4.   First Words
  5.   First Sentences

B.       Characteristics of Early Speech

C.       Classic Theories of Language Acquisition: The Nature-Nurture Debate

D.       Influences on Language Development
  1.   Maturation of the Brain
  2.   Social Interaction
  3.   Child-Directed Speech

E.       Preparing for Literacy: The Benefits of Reading Aloud

IMPORTANT TERMS FOR SECTION III

**Completion:** Fill in the blanks to complete the definitions of key terms for this section of Chapter 7.

1.  **language:** _____ system based on words and grammar.
2.  **literacy:** Ability to read and _____.
3.  **prelinguistic speech:** Forerunner of linguistic speech; utterance of sounds that are not _____. Includes crying, cooing, babbling, and accidental and deliberate imitation of sounds without understanding their meaning.
4.  **linguistic speech:** Verbal expression designed to convey _____.
5.  **holophrase:** _____ _____ that conveys a complete thought.
6.  _____-mixing: Use of elements of two languages, sometimes in the same utterance, by young children in households where both languages are spoken.
7.  _____ speech: Early form of sentence consisting of only a few essential words.
8.  **syntax:** Rules for forming _____ in a particular language.
9.  _____: Theory that human beings have an inborn capacity for language acquisition.
10. **language acquisition device (LAD):** In _____'s terminology, an inborn mechanism that enables children to infer linguistic rules from the language they hear.
11. **child-directed speech (CDS):** Form of speech often used in talking to babies or toddlers; includes slow, simplified speech, a high-pitched tone, exaggerated vowel sounds, short words and sentences, and much repetition. Also called _____.

## LEARNING OBJECTIVES FOR SECTION III

After reading and reviewing this section of Chapter 7, you should be able to do the following.

1. List in sequence at least six milestones in language development during the first 3 years.

2. Identify, in order of their emergence, four forms of early vocalization, or prelinguistic speech.

3. Trace the development of recognition of language sounds during the first year.

4. Explain the role of gestures in language development, identify three types of gestures, and give an example of each.

5. Distinguish between passive and active (or expressive) vocabulary, and describe how vocabulary grows during the single-word stage of linguistic speech.

6. Name four types of words commonly spoken during the single-word stage, and explain how contextual influences affect choice of words.

7. Describe the growth of language ability from the time children use their first sentences to approximately age 3.

8. Contrast the views of learning theorists and nativists, identify the single most important factor in language acquisition according to each theory, and discuss research that supports and challenges each.

9. Describe how deaf babies' acquire language, and discuss whether these findings support nativism or learning theory.

10. Cite evidence for genetic and temperamental influences on linguistic progress.

11. Describe ways in which parents' or caregivers' verbal interactions with babies play a role in each stage of language development.

12. Identify two contrasting models regarding the source of the impetus for linguistic progress.

13. Discuss how parents' socioeconomic status and other factors influence their style of speaking to their children, and how these speaking styles in turn influence children's vocabulary.

14. Discuss the influence of child-directed speech ("parentese") on language development and assess the pros and cons of its use.

15. Describe an effective technique for fostering toddlers' preliteracy skills.

## CHAPTER 7 QUIZ

**Matching**--Who's Who: Match each name in the left-hand column with the appropriate description at the right. (Note: Here, a description may be used to identify more than one name.)

1. Andrew Meltzoff _____

2. Noam Chomsky _____

3. Theodore Simon _____

4. Renée Baillargeon _____

5. Jean Piaget _____

6. Karen Wynn _____

7. M. Keith Moore _____

8. B. F. Skinner _____

9. Alfred Binet _____

10. Burton L. White _____

a.  studied mothers' influence on preschoolers' competence

b.  devised an early psychometric intelligence test

c.  used Mickey Mouse dolls to test infants' ability to "compute"

d.  studied the development of infants' reasoning about movements of objects

e.  foremost proponent of learning theory of language acquisition

f.  proposed the existence of an inborn language acquisition device

g.  formulated a stage theory of cognitive development based on observation of children

h.  conducted experiments on invisible and deferred imitation in very young infants

**Multiple-Choice:** Circle the choice that best completes or answers each item.

1. Which approach to cognitive development attempts to measure intelligence quantitatively?
    a. behaviorist
    b. psychometric
    c. Piagetian
    d. information-processing

2. As a baby sucks on a dry nipple, an experimenter plays a tape of a woman singing a lullaby. When the baby stops sucking, the singing stops; when the baby resumes sucking, the singing resumes. This is an example of
    a. habituation
    b. classical conditioning
    c. operant conditioning
    d. complex learning

3. Studies of 2- to 6-month-old babies whose kicking activates a mobile have found all but which of the following?
    a. Infants remember to kick when they see the mobile again a few days later.
    b. Infants remember to kick only if their legs are attached to the mobile.
    c. Infants are likely to kick if they see another moving object.
    d. Infants are more likely to kick when retested in similar surroundings.

4. Which of the following can reliably predict an infant's later intelligence?
    a. Stanford-Binet Intelligence Scale
    b. Bayley Scales of Infant Development
    c. both a and b
    d. neither a nor b

5. HOME (the Home Observation for Measurement of the Environment) has found a combination of all but which of the following fairly reliable in predicting children's IQ?
    a. parents' responsiveness
    b. parents' educational level
    c. socioeconomic status
    d. parents' involvement in children's play

6. Developmental priming mechanisms include all but which of the following?
    a. mentoring in basic skills
    b. celebration of accomplishments
    c. protection from inappropriate punishment
    d. close parental supervision

7. Babies tend to become more competent when given
    a. strict rules regarding orderliness
    b. as much parental attention as possible
    c. freedom to explore
    d. all of the above

8. At age 15, at-risk children who had participated in Partners for Learning, an early intervention program, during their preschool years
    a. had IQs equal to or better than the average for the general population
    b. had lost their early IQ gains and did no better than a control group
    c. had lower IQs than at age 3, but higher IQs than a control group
    d. had lower IQs than a control group

9. Which of the following is not something babies learn to do during the sensorimotor stage, according to Piaget?
    a. organize their behavior toward goals
    b. solve simple problems
    c. coordinate sensory information
    d. form lasting memories of events

10. In Piaget's terminology, thumb-sucking by a 2-month-old baby is a
    a. primary circular reaction
    b. secondary circular reaction
    c. tertiary circular reaction
    d. form of deferred imitation

11. According to Piaget, a 9-month-old baby who sees a toy on the floor, crawls to it, and picks it up is showing
    a. an acquired adaptation
    b. a tertiary circular reaction
    c. coordination of secondary schemes
    d. object permanence

12. According to Piaget, the approximate age at which babies typically begin to think is
    a. 8 months
    b. 12 months
    c. 15 months
    d. 18 months

13. According to Piaget, a 10-month-old baby who plays peekaboo is developing the concept of
    a. object permanence
    b. causality
    c. invisible imitation
    d. circular reactions

14. Research has challenged Piaget's estimate of the age at which children develop all but which of the following abilities?
    a. object permanence
    b. invisible imitation
    c. understanding of number
    d. trial-and-error problem solving
15. An infant's later intelligence shows a modest correlation with his or her
    a. speed of habituation
    b. visual recognition memory
    c. visual novelty preference
    d. all of the above
16. Violation-of-expectations research shows that 4½-month-old infants
    a. recognize their ability to act on their environment but do not know that outside forces can have causal effects
    b. can distinguish between events that flow into other events and events with no apparent cause
    c. have developed cross-modal transfer
    d. know that an inadequately supported object will fall
17. Cognitive neuroscience attributes infants' visual novelty preference to
    a. preexplicit memory
    b. explicit memory
    c. implicit memory
    d. working memory
18. Object permanence seems to depend on the development of
    a. preexplicit memory
    b. explicit memory
    c. implicit memory
    d. working memory
19. The social-contextual approach is chiefly concerned with
    a. The relationship between parental responsiveness and children's intelligence
    b. Parents' ability to create a stimulating home environment
    c. Parents' involvement in children's play
    d. The ways adults participate in children's learning

20. In a cross-cultural study based on Vygotsky's theory, caregivers in which of the following places gave much verbal instruction to children?
    a. Mayan town in Guatemala
    b. tribal village in India
    c. Salt Lake City
    d. Turkish city
21. A baby's earliest means of communication is
    a. cooing
    b. babbling
    c. crying
    d. smiling
22. Babies lose their sensitivity to sounds not used in their native language by
    a. 2 to 4 months
    b. 4 to 6 months
    c. 10 to 12 months
    d. 14 to 16 months
23. A 12-month-old baby who reaches for a ball and says "da" is using
    a. a holophrase
    b. a symbolic gesture
    c. telegraphic speech
    d. manual babbling
24. Telegraphic speech
    a. is universal among 1- and 2-year-olds
    b. is a form of prelinguistic speech
    c. reflects the word order a child hears
    d. consists of holophrases
25. The sentence "Mama goed bye-bye" is an example of a young child's tendency to
    a. overregularize rules
    b. speak ungrammatically
    c. underextend word meanings
    d. overextend word meanings
26. According to the nativist view of language acquisition, children learn to speak their native language by
    a. imitating their parents and caregivers
    b. analyzing the language they hear and figuring out its rules
    c. repeating sounds that receive positive reinforcement
    d. all of the above
27. When Kayla and her father talk, Kayla starts most of the conversations, and her father tends to acknowledge or repeat what she said. This fits the
    a. scaffolding model
    b. intentionality model
    c. guided participation model
    d. referential model

28. Child-directed speech, or "parentese,"
    a. focuses on telling children what to do
    b. is most frequently used by working-class mothers
    c. is more common in the United States than in other cultures
    d. seems to help infants distinguish speech sounds
29. Parents or caregivers help 2-year-olds develop preliteracy skills when they do <u>all but which</u> of the following while reading to the children?
    a. ask yes-or-no questions
    b. correct wrong answers
    c. expand on the children's answers
    d. encourage the child to tell the story

**True or False?** In the blank following each item, write T (for true) or F (for false). In the space below each item, if the statement is false, rewrite it to make it true.

1. Maturation is essential to the development of speech. _____

2. Newborns can learn by classical conditioning. _____

3. Studies using operant conditioning have found that 2-month-old infants cannot remember past events. _____

4. Intelligence tests were originally developed to identify bright students. _____

5. The Bayley Scales of Infant Development can help diagnose a neurological deficit. _____

6. IQ tests taken at age 2 reliably predict intelligence test scores later in childhood. _____

7. Infants born with mental disabilities rarely show improvement in tested intelligence. _____

8. In studies based on the HOME scale, the home environment had at least as strong an influence on cognitive development as the mother's IQ. _____

9. According to research, parents who want to enhance their children's competence should direct their interests into constructive channels. _____

10. Project CARE and the Abecedarian Project found that home visits are vital to the success of an early intervention program. _____

11. According to Piaget, the sensorimotor stage typically lasts from birth to about 3 years of age. _____

12. According to Piaget, the first thing infants learn is to suck. _____

13. Between about 1 to 4 months, according to Piaget, babies begin to repeat pleasurable actions. _____

14. Research has confirmed Piaget's belief that children younger than about 18 months are not yet capable of forming mental representations. _____

15. Research has established that newborn babies have the ability to imitate facial expressions. _____

16. Fourteen-month-olds seem to be able to "read" behavioral cues to another person's food preferences. _____

17. According to information-processing research, some aspects of a child's mental development are fairly continuous from birth. _____

18. Habituation occurs when a baby responds to a new stimulus. _____

19. Newborns can distinguish between familiar and unfamiliar sounds. _____

20. Research suggests that babies as young as 5 months may have a rudimentary understanding of number. _____

21. Mothers' responsiveness when their babies are in distress is related to individual differences in later cognitive development. _____

22. Knowing how to throw a ball is an example of explicit memory. _____

23. According to social-contextual research in Guatemala, India, Turkey, and Salt Lake City, it is not adaptive for adult caregivers to be directly involved in children's play. _____

24. Accidental and deliberate imitation are forms of prelinguistic speech. _____

25. A baby who waves bye-bye is using a symbolic gesture. _____

26. A baby's first word is typically said between the ages of 10 and 14 months. _____

27. Babies understand many words they cannot yet use. _____

28. As babies attach meaning to sounds, they pay closer attention to fine auditory distinctions.

_____

29. When they begin to talk, babies in all cultures use mostly nouns at first. _____

30. Toddlers' speech is a simplified version of adult speech. _____

31. Deaf babies and hearing babies learn language in the same sequence of stages. _____

32. Repeating babies' babbled sounds slows their speech development by reinforcing meaningless utterances. _____

33. Parents can best foster young children's vocabulary development by giving them frequent requests and commands. _____

34. Infants prefer simplified speech. _____

35. Reading aloud to children at an early age can foster the growth of preliteracy skills. _____

# ANSWER KEY FOR CHAPTER 7

## CHAPTER 7 REVIEW

### Important Terms for Section I
1. intelligent
2. behaviorist
3. psychometric
4. Piagetian, Jean Piaget
5. classical
6. operant
7. quotient
8. representative
9. Bayley
10. cognitive
11. priming mechanisms
12. intervention
13. 2
14. structures
15. reactions
16. symbols
17. deferred
18. imaginary
19. sight
20. invisible
21. visible

### Important Terms for Section II
1. perceiving
2. activity
3. contextual
4. familiarity
5. responsiveness
6. stimulus
7. novelty
8. transfer
9. competence
10. surprising
11. another
12. explicit, implicit
13. implicit, explicit
14. short
15. guided

### Important Terms for Section III
1. communication
2. write
3. words
4. meaning
5. single word
6. code
7. telegraphic
8. sentences

9. nativism
10. Chomsky
11. parentese

## CHAPTER 7 QUIZ

### Matching--Who's Who
1. h
2. f
3. b
4. d
5. g
6. c
7. h
8. e
9. b
10. a

### Multiple-Choice
1. b
2. c
3. b
4. d
5. c
6. d
7. c
8. c
9. d
10. a
11. c
12. d
13. a
14. d
15. d
16. b
17. a
18. d
19. d
20. c
21. c
22. c
23. a
24. c
25. a
26. b
27. b
28. d
29. a

### True or False?
1. T
2. T

3. F-Research using operant conditioning shows that infants of 2 months can remember to repeat an action in similar circumstances.
4. F-Intelligence tests were originally developed to identify children who could not handle academic work.
5. T
6. F-Until close to age 5, IQ tests are unreliable as predictors of future scores.
7. F-A "self-righting tendency" enables some infants born with mental disabilities to show significant improvement in intelligence as they grow older.
8. T
9. F-Parents who want to enhance children's competence should talk to them about whatever they are interested in at the moment.
10. F-Home visits did not significantly affect the outcome.
11. F-The sensorimotor stage lasts from birth to about 2 years.
12. F-Infants are born with a sucking reflex; they learn to <u>use</u> sucking to meet their goals.
13. T
14. F-Some research suggests that infants can form mental representations much earlier than Piaget believed.
15. F-Research in which newborns appeared to imitate adult facial expressions has been replicated only with regard to sticking out the tongue, and alternative explanations have been advanced for this phenomenon.
16. F-Eighteen-month-olds, but not fourteen-month-olds, seem to be able to read another person's food preferences.
17. T
18. F-Habituation occurs when response to a familiar stimulus declines; dishabituation occurs when the baby responds to a new stimulus.
19. T
20. T
21. F-Mothers' responsiveness when babies are <u>not</u> in distress is related to later cognitive development.
22. F-Knowing how to throw a ball is an example of implicit memory.
23. According to this research, the adaptiveness of adult involvement in children's play depends on the cultural context.
24. T
25. F-A baby who waves bye-bye is using a conventional social gesture.
26. T
27. T
28. F-As babies try to attach meanings to sounds, they temporarily pay less attention to fine auditory distinctions.
29. F-The kinds of words babies initially use seem to depend on the structure of their native language and on the social context in which they hear it.
30. F-Toddlers' speech is not just a simplified version of adult speech; it has its own special characteristics.
31. T
32. F-Repeating babies' babbled sounds helps them experience the social aspect of speech.
33. F-Children learn new words faster when caregivers give or ask for information than when they give request or commands.
34. T
35. T

# CHAPTER 8
# PSYCHOSOCIAL DEVELOPMENT DURING THE FIRST THREE YEARS

## OVERVIEW

Chapter 8 begins the exploration of psychosocial development with themes that continue, with variations, at each stage of childhood. In this chapter, the authors:

❑ Report what is known about infants' emotions and how they show these emotions

❑ Discuss the early influences of temperament and the family

❑ Present Erikson's theoretical perspectives on the development of trust, the "crisis" of infancy, and autonomy, the "crisis" of toddlerhood.

❑ Describe research on the development of attachment, of emotional communication with caregivers, of stranger anxiety and separation anxiety, and of social referencing.

❑ Explore developmental issues of toddlerhood, including the emergence of the sense of self, internalization of societal rules, and the origins of conscience.

❑ Describe interactions with siblings and other children

❑ Assess the impact of early day care on cognitive, emotional, and social development, and identify characteristics of high quality day care

## GUIDEPOSTS FOR STUDY

8.1 When and how do emotions develop and how do babies show them?

8.2 How do infants show temperamental differences and how enduring are those differences?

8.3 What roles do mothers and fathers play in early personality development?

8.4 How do infants gain trust in their world and for attachments?

8.5 How do infants and caregivers "read" each other's nonverbal signals?

8.6 When does the sense of self arise and what are three steps in its development?

8.7 How do toddlers develop autonomy and standards for socially acceptable behavior?

8.8 How do infants and toddlers interact with siblings and other children?

8.9 How do parental employment and early childcare affect infant and toddler development?

## CHAPTER 8 REVIEW

**Section I Foundations of Psychosocial Development**

FRAMEWORK FOR SECTION I

A.   Emotions
   1.   Early Signs of Emotion
   2.   When Do Various Emotions Develop?
   3.   Brain Growth and Emotional Development

B.    Temperament
    1.    Aspects and Patterns of Temperament: New York Longitudinal Study
    2.    Effects of Temperament on Adjustment: "Goodness of Fit"
    3.    How is Temperament Measured?
    4.    How Stable is Temperament?
    5.    Biological Bases of temperament
    6.    Cross-Cultural differences

C.    Earliest Social Experiences: The Infant in the Family
    1.    The Mother's Role
    2.    The Father's Role
    3.    How Parents Shape Gender Differences
    4.    Grandparent's Role

## IMPORTANT TERMS FOR SECTION I

**Completion:** Fill in the blanks to complete the definitions of key terms for this section of Chapter 8.

1.  **emotions:** _____ feelings such as sadness, joy, and fear, which arise in response to situations and experiences and are expressed through altered behavior.
2.  **self-**_____: Realization that one's existence is separate from other people and things.
3.  _____: Person's characteristic disposition, or style of approaching and reacting to people and situations.
4.  _____ **children:** Children with a generally happy temperament, regular biological rhythms, and a readiness to accept new experiences.
5.  _____ **children:** Children with irritable temperament, irregular biological rhythms, and intense emotional responses.
6.  ____ - __ - _____ - ___ **children:** Children whose temperament is generally mild but who are hesitant about accepting new experiences.
7.  **goodness of fit:** Appropriateness of environmental demands and constraints to a child's _____.
8.  **gender-**_____: Socialization process by which children, at an early age, learn behavior deemed appropriate by the culture for a boy or girl.

## LEARNING OBJECTIVES FOR SECTION I

After reading and reviewing this section of Chapter 8, you should be able to do the following.

1.  Tell how researchers study babies' emotions; name at least five emotions babies seem to show during the first year; and explain the relationship between self-awareness and the development of emotions.

2.  Identify four patterns of crying, and explain the value of crying as a diagnostic tool.

3. Trace changes, with age, in what makes babies smile and laugh.

4. Describe three temperamental patterns, and tell how temperament is assessed.

5. Explain the significance of "goodness of fit" and its implications for parenting.

6. Discuss influences on, and stability of, temperament.

7. Identify societal changes and cultural patterns in family life that affect children's socialization, and cite two current trends in research on the family's influence on personality development.

8.  Point out the significance of Harlow's research on monkeys separated from their mothers after birth.

9.  Compare infants' interactions with their mothers and with their fathers, and discuss the significance of the father-infant relationship, especially with regard to gender-typing.

10. Summarize what is known about physical, cognitive, and psychosocial differences between baby boys and girls.

11. Describe two common patterns of grandparenting, and discuss the importance of the grandparent's role.

**Section II Developmental Issues in Infancy**

FRAMEWORK FOR SECTION II

A.   Developing Trust

B.   Developing Attachments
    1.   Studying Patterns of Attachment
    2.   How Attachment Is Established
    3.   The Role of Temperament
    4.   Intergenerational Transmission of Attachment Patterns
    5.   Stranger Anxiety and Separation Anxiety
    6.   Long-Term Effects of Attachment

C.   Emotional Communication with Caregivers: Mutual Regulation
    1.   How a Mother's Depression Affects Mutual Regulation

D.   Social Referencing

## IMPORTANT TERMS FOR SECTION II

**Completion:** Fill in the blanks to complete the definitions of key terms for this section of Chapter 8.

1. _____ _____ **versus** _____ _____: In Erikson's theory, the first crisis in psychosocial development, occurring between birth and about 18 months, in which infants develop a sense of the reliability of people and objects in their world.

2. **attachment:** Reciprocal, enduring relationship between _____ and caregiver, each of whom contributes to the quality of the relationship.

3. _____ **Situation:** Laboratory technique used to study attachment.

4. _____ **attachment:** Attachment pattern in which an infant separates readily from the primary caregiver and actively seeks out the caregiver upon the caregiver's return.

5. _____ **attachment:** Attachment pattern in which an infant rarely cries when separated from the primary caregiver and avoids contact upon his or her return.

6. _____ **(resistant) attachment:** Attachment pattern in which an infant becomes anxious before the primary caregiver leaves, is extremely upset during his or her absence, and both seeks and resists contact on his or her return.

7. _____ **attachment:** Attachment pattern in which an infant, after being separated from the primary caregiver, shows contradictory behaviors upon his or her return.

8. **Attachment Q-Set (AQS):** Instrument for measuring attachment, developed by Waters and Deane, in which observer sorts descriptive words and phrases into those most and least characteristic of a child and compares these descriptors with descriptions of the "hypothetical most _____ child."

9. **Preschool Assessment of Attachment (PAA):** Instrument for measuring attachment after 20 months of age, which takes into account the complexity of preschoolers' relationships and _____ abilities.

10. **Adult Attachment Interview (AAI):** Instrument for measuring the clarity, coherence, and _____ of an adult's memories of attachment to her or his parents.

11. _____ _____: Process by which infant and caregiver communicate emotional states to each other and respond appropriately.

12. _____: Affective disorder in which a person feels unhappy and often has trouble eating, sleeping, and concentrating.

13. _____ **anxiety:** Wariness of strange people and places, shown by some infants during the second half of the first year.

14. _____ **anxiety:** Distress shown by an infant when a familiar caregiver leaves.

15. **social** _____: Understanding an ambiguous situation by seeking out another person's perception of it.

## LEARNING OBJECTIVES FOR SECTION II

After reading and reviewing this section of Chapter 8, you should be able to do the following.

1. Describe the first crisis proposed by Erik Erikson, basic trust versus basic mistrust.

2. Trace the development of an infant's early attachment behavior.

3. Describe and evaluate the Strange Situation and other instruments for research on attachment.

4. Identify four patterns of attachment; discuss how these patterns are established, influences upon them, and their long-term effects.

5. Describe research on the mutual regulation model and its relevance to babies' emotional development.

6. Tell how a mother's depression can affect her baby, and name several effective interventions.

7. Identify factors influencing stranger anxiety and separation anxiety.

8. Discuss whether or not infants exhibit social referencing.

## Section III Developmental Issues in Toddlerhood

### FRAMEWORK FOR SECTION III

A. The Emerging Sense of Self

B. Developing Autonomy

C. Socialization and Internalization: Developing a Conscience
  1. Developing Self-Regulation
  2. Origins of Conscience: Committed Compliance
  3. Factors in the Success of Socialization

### IMPORTANT TERMS FOR SECTION III

**Completion:** Fill in the blanks to complete the definitions of key terms for this section of Chapter 8.

1. **self-concept:** Sense of self; descriptive and evaluative mental picture of one's abilities and _____.
2. _____ **versus** _____ _____: In Erikson's theory, the second crisis in psychosocial development, occurring between about 18 months and 3 years, in which children achieve a balance between self-determination and control by others.
3. _____: Behavior characteristic of toddlers, in which they express their desire for independence by resisting authority.
4. **socialization:** Process of developing the habits, skills, values, and motives shared by responsible, productive members of a particular _____.
5. _____: Process by which children accept societal standards of conduct as their own; fundamental to socialization.
6. **self-regulation:** Child's independent control of behavior to conform to understood social _____.
7. **conscience:** _____ standards of behavior, which usually control one's conduct and produce emotional discomfort when violated.
8. _____ **compliance:** In Kochanska's terminology, a toddler's wholehearted obedience of a parent's orders without reminders or lapses.
9. _____ **compliance:** In Kochanska's terminology, a toddler's obedience of a parent's orders only in the presence of prompting or other signs of ongoing parental control.
10. **reciprocity:** In Maccoby's terminology, system of _____ binding, _____ responsive relationships into which a child is socialized.

### LEARNING OBJECTIVES FOR SECTION III

After reading and reviewing this section of Chapter 8, you should be able to do the following.

1. Trace three stages in the development of the self-concept during infancy and toddlerhood.

2. Describe the second crisis proposed by Erik Erikson, autonomy versus shame and doubt.

3. List at least four suggestions for dealing with toddlers' negativism and developing socially acceptable behavior.

4. Discuss the development of self-regulation and its relationship to socialization and internalization.

5. Assess the relationship of committed compliance and situational compliance to the development of conscience.

6. Identify factors that influence the success of socialization.

**Section IV Contact With Other Children**

FRAMEWORK FOR SECTION IV

A.     Siblings
      1.   The Arrival of a New Baby
      2.   How Siblings Interact

B.     Sociability with Nonsiblings


LEARNING OBJECTIVES FOR SECTION IV

After reading and reviewing this section of Chapter 8, you should be able to do the following.

1.  Describe typical reactions to the arrival of a new baby and suggest ways to help siblings adjust.




2.  Describe the complex interactions between siblings during infancy and toddlerhood.




3.  Trace changes in typical social interactions among infants and toddlers, and cite influences on individual differences in sociability




**Section V Children of Working Parents**

FRAMEWORK FOR SECTION V

A.     Effect of Parental employment

B.     The Impact of Early child Care


LEARNING OBJECTIVES FOR SECTION V

After reading and reviewing this section of Chapter 8, you should be able to do the following.

1.  Identify trends in child care and characteristics of good day care.




2.  Discuss findings on the impact of early day care on cognitive, emotional, and social development.

# CHAPTER 8 QUIZ

**Matching--Who's Who:** Match each name in the left-hand column with the appropriate description at the right. (Note: Here, a description may be used for more than one name.)

1. Mary Ainsworth _____

2. Stella C. Chess _____

3. Herbert B. Birch _____

4. Carroll Izard _____

5. Margaret Mead _____

6. Harry and Margaret Harlow _____

7. Grazyna Kochanska _____

8. Eleanor Maccoby _____

9. Erik H. Erikson _____

10. Alexander T. Thomas _____

11. René Spitz _____

a. studied the origins of conscience
b. proposed reciprocity model of socialization
c. studied own baby's psychosocial development
d. pioneered in attachment research employing the Strange Situation
e. traced temperamental traits from infancy to young adulthood
f. described achievement of basic trust in infancy and of autonomy in toddlerhood
g. studied mothering needs of infant rhesus monkeys
h. studied effects of early institutionalization
i. studied infants' emotions by observing their facial expressions

**Multiple-Choice:** Circle the choice that best completes or answers each item.

1. Which of the following emotions does <u>not</u> seem to appear during the first year?
   a. anger
   b. guilt
   c. fear
   d. surprise

2. An infant suddenly begins to cry loudly and then holds her breath. This is which pattern of crying?
   a. hunger cry
   b. pain cry
   c. frustration cry
   d. angry cry

3. The earliest smile of newborns is produced by
   a. gas
   b. pleasure
   c. recognition of parents
   d. spontaneous nervous system activity

4. <u>All but which</u> of the following are probably attributable to temperament?
   a. insomnia
   b. frequent constipation
   c. creativity
   d. cheerfulness

5. Which of the following 3-year-olds is likely to be best adjusted?
   a. Abbie, an "easy" child whose parents are in the midst of a contested divorce
   b. Ben, a "slow-to-warm-up" child whose family has had to move four times because of job changes
   c. Carol, a "difficult" child whose parents feed her on a flexible schedule
   d. none of the above; temperament is not a major factor in adjustment

6. Research suggests that temperamental differences are influenced by
   a. heredity
   b. parental treatment
   c. both a and b
   d. neither a nor b

7. Experiments with rhesus monkeys, raised in cages with plain and cloth-covered wire-mesh surrogate "mothers," produced <u>all but which</u> of the following conclusions?
   a. Baby monkeys cling more to a surrogate "mother" that provides soft bodily contact than to one that feeds them.
   b. Baby monkeys will not take food from an inanimate "mother."
   c. Baby monkeys raised with inanimate "mothers" do not grow up normally.
   d. Baby monkeys remember a cloth surrogate "mother" better than a plain wire one.

8. Which of the following statements about fathers' relationships with their babies is true?
   a. Fathers promote gender-typing more than mothers do.
   b. Fathers spend less time playing with their babies than mothers do.
   c. Fathers' tendency to be less responsive than mothers is biologically based.
   d. In all cultures, fathers' style of playing with their babies is vigorous and highly physical.

9. Differences between infant boys' and girls' personalities
   a. are evident almost from birth
   b. reflect physiological differences between the sexes
   c. may reflect different treatment by adults
   d. show up consistently in a number of studies

10. Which of the following grandparents is likely to spend the most time with a grandchild?
   a. 50-year-old African American living out of town
   b. 72-year-old African American with teenage grandchild
   c. 55-year-old white, estranged from child's mother
   d. 65-year-old white living in the same city

11. Erikson maintained that the resolution of the crisis of trust versus mistrust occurs primarily in
   a. the first few hours after birth
   b. the period from 18 months to three years of age
   c. the feeding situation
   d. toilet training

12. Research suggests that the least securely attached babies may be those whose attachment pattern is characterized as
   a. disorganized-disoriented
   b. ambivalent
   c. avoidant
   d. resistant

13. Which of the following was the earliest instrument for measuring attachment?
   a. Strange Situation
   b. Attachment Q-Set
   c. Preschool Assessment of Attachment
   d. Adult Attachment Interview

14. Which of the following has been identified as a probable factor in security of attachment?
   a. number of siblings close in age
   b. normal hearing in the baby
   c. mother's employment
   d. mother's memory of her early attachment to her own mother

15. Which of the following involves a baby's "reading" a caregiver's behavior or expression and adjusting his or her own behavior accordingly?
   a. mutual regulation model
   b. social referencing
   c. both a and b
   d. neither a nor b

16. The "still-face" paradigm is used to assess
   a. security of attachment
   b. mutual regulation
   c. stranger anxiety
   d. social referencing

17. Babies of severely or chronically depressed mothers tend to do all but which of the following?
   a. comfort themselves by rocking or sucking
   b. act upset when separated from the mother
   c. show poor cognitive development
   d. become depressed themselves

18. Stranger anxiety seems to be related to all but which of the following?
   a. insecure attachment
   b. temperament
   c. cultural patterns
   d. caregiver's reaction to the stranger

19. As 12-month-old Emily plays in the sandbox, her mother sits nearby on a park bench. When another woman sits down on the bench, Emily looks at her mother uncertainly. Only after Emily sees her mother give the woman a friendly greeting does Emily smile and resume playing. This seems to be an example of
   a. internalization
   b. separation anxiety
   c. insecure attachment
   d. social referencing

20. Which of the following stages of self-concept development comes first?
   a. self-recognition
   b. self-description
   c. self-evaluation
   d. self-regulation

21. According to Erikson, the "virtue" that should emerge during toddlerhood is
    a. will
    b. hope
    c. self-determination
    d. trust
22. Language is a key factor in personality development during Erikson's crisis of
    a. basic trust versus basic mistrust
    b. autonomy versus shame and doubt
    c. mutual regulation versus self-regulation
    d. independence versus negativism
23. Which of the following does not seem to be a precursor of conscience?
    a. inhibitory control
    b. committed compliance
    c. situational compliance
    d. concern with flawed objects
24. All but which of the following statements about sibling relationships in infancy and toddlerhood are true?
    a. Most behavioral problems of older siblings disappear by the time a new baby is 8 months old.
    b. Young children become attached to older brothers and sisters.
    c. Siblings who are farther apart in age tend to fight more.
    d. Two-year-olds often tease older siblings.
25. Which of the following is not necessarily a criterion of good day care?
    a. small groups of children
    b. college-educated caregivers
    c. child-related training of caregivers
    d. high staff-child ratio
26. When tested for intelligence and on other cognitive measures, 2-to-4-year-olds in good day care centers
    a. Score slightly lower than home-raised children.
    b. Score significantly lower than home-raised children.
    c. Score as high or higher than home-raised children, but this gain is often temporary.
    d. Appear to attain a permanent advantage over home-raised children.
27. In research on children in a semirural area who entered day care before the age of 8 months, which of the following was a better predictor of social adjustment?
    a. age of entry
    b. quality of care
    c. hours spent in care
    d. All were equally good predictors .

**True or False?** In the blank following each statement, write T (for true) or F (for false). In the space below each statement, if the statement is false, rewrite it to make it true.

1. One of the first emotions infants show is disgust. _____

2. Babies whose parents regularly respond to their cries tend to become more dependent. _____

3. An 8-month-old baby may laugh at something unexpected. _____

4. An "easy" child is one who is easy to raise. _____

5. Temperament tends to be stable. _____

118

6. Efe infants are breastfed by other women in addition to their mothers. _____

7. Gender-typed behavior increases throughout the preschool period. _____

8. Most grandparents are deeply involved in their grandchildren's lives. _____

9. According to Erikson, it is important to avoid creating mistrust in an infant. _____

10. According to Ainsworth, an essential part of human personality development is an infant's attachment to the mother _____

11. Ainsworth found that attachment to the mother generally develops by 6 or 7 months. _____

12. Infants who are securely attached to the mother tend to stay by her side. _____

13. Research has found that mothers' employment has a negative effect on babies' security of attachment. _____

14. Babies who are securely attached to their mothers also tend to be securely attached to their fathers. _____

15. During the "still-face" episode, infants usually engage in attention-seeking behaviors. _____

16. Babies of depressed mothers tend to show signs of emotional withdrawal because of inability to elicit responses from the mother. _____

17. Stranger anxiety is universal across cultures. _____

18. By 18 months, babies typically can recognize their own image. _____

19. Negativism generally peaks at about age 3½ to 4. _____

20. Self-regulation is generally developed by the age of 2. _____

21. Children whose mothers closely supervise their compliance with household rules tend to obey more readily than children who are less closely supervised. _____

22. Sibling conflict increases when the younger sibling becomes a toddler. _____

23. Babies become more sociable around the age of 1 year, when they start to walk. _____

24. In the United States, children from low-income families tend to receive the worst quality of care in organized day care centers. _____

25. Early entrance into day care negatively affects security of attachment. _____

## ANSWER KEY FOR CHAPTER 8

### CHAPTER 8 REVIEW

#### Important Terms for Section I
1. subjective
2. awareness
3. temperament
4. easy
5. difficult
6. slow-to-warm-up
7. temperament
8. typing

#### Important Terms for Section II
1. basic trust, basic mistrust
2. infant
3. Strange
4. secure
5. avoidant
6. ambivalent
7. disorganized-disoriented
8. secure
9. linguistic
10. consistency
11. mutual regulation
12. depression
13. stranger
14. separation
15. referencing

#### Important Terms for Section III
1. traits
2. autonomy, shame and doubt
3. negativism
4. society
5. internalization
6. expectations
7. internal
8. committed
9. situational
10. mutually, mutually

### CHAPTER 8 QUIZ

#### Matching--Who's Who
1. d
2. e
3. e
4. i
5. c
6. g
7. a
8. b
9. f
10. e
11. h

#### Multiple-Choice
1. b
2. b
3. d
4. c
5. c
6. c
7. b
8. a
9. c
10. a
11. c
12. a
13. a
14. d
15. c
16. b
17. b
18. a
19. d
20. a
21. a
22. b
23. c
24. c
25. b
26. c
27. b

#### True or False?
1. T
2. F-Babies whose cries bring a response gain a sense of connection with other people and control over their world.
3. T
4. F-No temperamental type is immune to behavioral problems; a key factor is "goodness of

fit" between the child's temperament and the demands made on the child.

5. T
6. T
7. According to one study, gender differences in play, and parental promotion of them, are greater at 18 months than at 5 years.
8. F-Most grandparents are frequent, casual companions to their grandchildren but are not deeply involved in their upbringing.
9. F-According to Erikson, although trust predominates in a healthy personality, some degree of mistrust is necessary for children to learn to protect themselves.
10. F-According to Ainsworth, an essential part of human personality development appears to be an infant's attachment to a mother figure--the mother or another caregiver.
11. T
12. F-Infants who are securely attached tend to use the mother as a secure base for exploration.
13. F-Research on the relationship between mothers' employment and babies' security of attachment suggests that the mother's feelings about working, not the fact of employment itself, may affect attachment.
14. T

15. F-During the "still-face" episode, infants usually stop trying to make contact with the mother and engage in self-comforting behaviors.
16. T
17. F-There are cross-cultural differences in stranger anxiety.
18. T
19. T
20. F-Self-regulation typically does not fully develop until at least age 3.
21. Children who are closely supervised tend to show less committed compliance, and are less likely to internalize adult rules.
22. T
23. F-Babies become less sociable around the age of 1 year, when they start to walk; their interest at that age becomes more focused on manipulating objects.
24. F- Children from middle-income families tend to receive worse quality of care, because they do not benefit from federal subsidies.
25. F. Early entrance into day care has no direct, independent effect on attachment.

# PHYSICAL DEVELOPMENT AND HEALTH IN EARLY CHILDHOOD

## OVERVIEW

Chapter 9 covers physical development and health in the preschool years between ages 3 and 6. In this chapter, the authors:

❑ Describe preschool children's physical growth and change and summarize their nutritional needs

❑ Identify normal sleep patterns and common sleep problems

❑ Trace the development of motor and artistic skills and discuss the significance of handedness

❑ Point out health issues that may arise during these predominantly healthy years, and environmental factors that may contribute to health problems

❑ Discuss causes and effects of child abuse and neglect and methods of prevention and treatment

## GUIDEPOSTS FOR STUDY

9.1   How do children's bodies change between ages 3 and 6 and what are their nutritional and dental needs?

9.2   What sleep patterns and problems tend to develop during early childhood?

9.3   What are the main motor achievements of early childhood and how does artwork done by children show their physical and cognitive maturation?

9.4   What are the major health and safety risks for children?

9.5   What are the causes and consequences of child abuse and neglect and what can be done about it?

## CHAPTER 9 REVIEW

**Section I Aspects of Physiological Development**

FRAMEWORK FOR SECTION I

A.      Bodily Growth and Change

B.      Nutrition

C.      Oral Health

D.      Sleep Patterns and Problems

      1.   Sleep Disturbances and Disorders

      2.   Bed-Wetting

## IMPORTANT TERMS FOR SECTION I

**Completion:** Fill in the blanks to complete the definitions of the key terms for this section of Chapter 9.

  1. _____ **objects:** Objects used repeatedly by a child as bedtime companions.

  2. **enuresis:** Repeated _____ in clothing or in bed.

## LEARNING OBJECTIVES FOR SECTION I

After reading and reviewing this section of Chapter 9, you should be able to do the following.

1. Summarize how boys and girls change in appearance, height, and weight between ages 3 and 6.

2. Summarize dental development in early childhood and appropriate treatment for thumb-sucking.

3. Discuss nutritional needs and prevention of obesity in early childhood.

4. List at least five suggestions for helping children eat and sleep well.

5. Describe normal sleep patterns and bedtime routines of preschoolers.

6. Name and describe three kinds of sleep disturbances, and tell how they should be treated.

7. Identify factors that may be involved in bed-wetting and effective ways of treating it.

**Section II Motor Development**

## FRAMEWORK FOR SECTION II

A.  Gross Motor Skills
B.  Fine Motor Skills and Artistic Development
C.  Handedness

## IMPORTANT TERMS FOR SECTION II

**Completion:** Fill in the blanks to complete the definitions of key terms for this section of Chapter 9.

1. _____ **skills:** Physical skills that involve the large muscles.
2. _____ **skills:** Physical skills that involve the small muscles and eye-hand coordination.
3. **systems of** _____: Combinations of motor skills that permit increasingly complex activities.
4. **handedness:** _____ for using a particular hand.

## LEARNING OBJECTIVES FOR SECTION II

After reading and reviewing this section of Chapter 9, you should be able to do the following.

1. Outline the development of gross motor skills, explain what causes that development, and suggest appropriate ways to foster it.

2. Give examples of advances in fine motor skills.

3. Summarize gender differences in young children's strength, musculature, coordination, and motor skills.

4. Discuss possible causes of handedness, cultural attitudes toward it, and advantages and disadvantages of being left- or right-handed.

5. Outline four stages in young children's drawing and tell how Rhoda Kellogg suggests adults can best encourage children's artistic development.

6. Explain how art therapy can help children deal with emotional trauma.

## Section III Health and Safety
## FRAMEWORK FOR SECTION III
A.     Minor Illnesses
B.     Accidental Injuries
C.     Health in Context: Environmental Influences
     1.  Exposure to Illness
     2.  Exposure to Smoking
     3.  Poverty
     4.  Exposure to Lead

## LEARNING OBJECTIVES FOR SECTION III
After reading and reviewing this section of Chapter 9, you should be able to do the following.
1. Summarize current trends in death rates from major childhood illnesses.

2. Tell the physical, cognitive, and emotional benefits of frequent minor respiratory illnesses in young children.

3. Identify the two most common causes and the two most common sites of accidents fatal to young children; discuss the effectiveness of laws aimed at preventing such accidents; and list recommended precautions for reducing the risk of accidents.

4. Discuss how exposure to smoking, illness and stress, poverty and homelessness, and lead may affect young children's health and well-being.

## Section IV Maltreatment: Abuse and Neglect
### FRAMEWORK FOR SECTION IV

A.      Maltreatment: Facts and Figures
B.      Contributing Factors: An Ecological View
    1.   Characteristics of Abusive Parents
    2.   Neighborhood and Social Support
    3.   Cultural Values and Patterns
C.      Effects of Maltreatment
D.      Helping Families in Trouble or at Rick

### IMPORTANT TERMS FOR SECTION IV

**Completion:** Fill in the blanks to complete the definitions of key terms for this section of Chapter 9.

1. **physical abuse:** Action taken to endanger a child involving potential injury to the _____.
2. _____ _____ **syndrome:** Condition showing symptoms of physical abuse of a child.
3. **physical** _____: Failure to meet a child's basic needs, such as food, clothing, medical care, protection, and supervision.
4. **Sexual abuse:** Sexual contact between a child and a[n] _____ person.
5. **emotional (psychological) abuse:** _____ action that may damage children's behavioral, cognitive, emotional, or physical functioning.
6. **emotional (psychological) neglect:** _____ to give a child emotional support, love, and affection.

### LEARNING OBJECTIVES FOR SECTION IV

After reading and reviewing this section of Chapter 9, you should be able to do the following.

1. Distinguish among physical abuse, sexual abuse, emotional abuse, and physical and emotional neglect.

2. Summarize trends in the incidence of maltreatment, and explain why its incidence is hard to measure.

3. Describe typical characteristics of abusive and neglectful parents.

4. Identify typical characteristics of children who are especially likely to be victims of abuse.

5. State ways in which community and culture may contribute to maltreatment of children.

6. Discuss the long-term effects of various types of maltreatment.

7. Describe effective ways of preventing maltreatment and of helping abused children and their families.

# CHAPTER 9 QUIZ

**Matching--Numbers:** Match each item at the left with the correct number in the right-hand column.

1. Approximate percentage of 5-year-old boys who are bed-wetters _____
2. Age at which all primary teeth are normally present _____
3. Age at which permanent teeth generally begin to appear _____
4. Number of primary teeth _____
5. Approximate percentage of African American children living in poverty _____
6. Number of scribble patterns a 2-year-old typically can draw _____
7. Average height in inches of a 6-year-old boy or girl _____
8. Percentage of U.S. children and adolescents whose diet meets none of the recommended guidelines _____
9. Age at which a child typically can hop four to six steps on one foot _____
10. Age at which a child typically can walk downstairs unaided, alternating feet _____

a.   3

b.   4

c.   5

d.   6

e.   7

f.   16

g.   17

h.   20

i.   37

j.   46

**Multiple-Choice:** Circle the choice that best completes or answers each item.

1. Which of the following would <u>not</u> be a normal change after age 3?
   a. faster growth rate
   b. more slender appearance
   c. increased stamina
   d. decreased appetite

2. Which of the following is <u>not</u> among suggestions that, according to your text, may help in dealing with young children who are finicky eaters?
   a. serving finger foods
   b. introducing new foods one at a time
   c. serving casseroles to "hide" rejected foods
   d. giving the child a choice of foods

3. Which of the following is (are) normal for preschoolers?
   a. prolonged bedtime struggles
   b. transitional objects
   c. frequent nightmares
   d. bed-wetting

4. Sleep terrors differ from nightmares in that sleep terrors
   a. usually occur within 1 hour after falling asleep
   b. are often remembered vividly
   c. are experienced more by girls than boys
   d. often follow a heavy meal before bedtime

5. According to the text, which of the following is <u>not</u> an effective treatment for bed-wetting?
   a. Teach the child to control the sphincter muscles.
   b. Wake a child who begins to urinate.
   c. Administer antidepressant drugs.
   d. Punish the child for wetting the bed.

6. Children between the ages of 3 and 6 advance in gross motor skills in part because their
   a. brain stem is better developed
   b. muscles, bones, and lungs are stronger
   c. reflexes are quicker
   d. eye-hand coordination is improved

7. Left-handed people tend to be
   a. long-lived
   b. poor in spatial tasks
   c. dyslexic
   d. ambidextrous

8. According to Kellogg, a child's purpose in drawing shapes and designs is to
   a. portray real objects
   b. develop eye-hand coordination
   c. explore form and design
   d. please parents and teachers

9. The leading cause of death among infants and children in the United States is
   a. cancer
   b. respiratory illnesses
   c. accidents
   d. AIDS
10. Most fatal injuries happen to children
   a. riding in motor vehicles
   b. struck by motor vehicles
   c. in day care center playgrounds
   d. in and around the home
11. Which of the following is the leading cause of death in children younger than 5?
   a. car crashes
   b. drowning
   c. fires
   d. passive smoking
12. Who of the following children is likely to be sick the least often?
   a. child in large day care center
   b. child in high quality day care
   c. child in large family, raised at home
   d. child in small family, raised at home
13. Stressful family events appear to increase children's susceptibility to
   a. illness
   b. injury
   c. both a and b
   d. neither a nor b
14. Children in poor families are at high risk of
   a. hearing loss
   b. insomnia
   c. lead poisoning
   d. all of the above
15. Who of the following is more likely to repeat a grade in school?
   a. middle-class child
   b. poor child living at home
   c. child whose family is homeless
   d. none of the above; no relationship between socioeconomic status or homelessness and school failure has been found
16. Children are most likely to be abused or neglected by
   a. foster parents
   b. day care staff
   c. their natural parents
   d. the mother's boyfriend

17. Approximately what proportion of abusive parents were abused themselves as children?
   a. 10 percent
   b. one-third
   c. half
   d. more than 90 percent
18. Which of the following is (are) not characteristic of abusive parents?
   a. marital problems and physical fighting
   b. disorganized household
   c. large number of children closely spaced
   d. emotional withdrawal from spouse and children
19. Victims of child abuse are likely to be
   a. passive and compliant
   b. cold and unaffectionate
   c. needy and demanding
   d. none of the above; the parent's personality, not the child's, determines the likelihood of abuse
20. Preschoolers who have been sexually abused are likely to
   a. have nightmares
   b. be hyperactive
   c. run away from home
   d. all of the above

**True or False?** In the blank following each item, write T (for true) or F (for false). In the space below each item, if the statement is false, rewrite it to make it true.

1. Boys at age 3 tend to be a little taller and heavier than girls. _____

2. To avoid permanent damage, thumb-sucking should be stopped before the deciduous teeth come in. _____

3. Preschoolers typically eat less in proportion to their size than infants do. _____

4. Enuresis runs in families. _____

5. Five-year-old boys tend to be better than 5-year-old girls at catching a ball _____

6. Handedness usually develops by age 3. _____

7. According to Rhoda Kellogg, adults should encourage children to draw more recognizable pictures. _____

8. By early childhood, the lungs are fully developed. _____

9. Children's death rates from major illnesses have decreased in recent years. _____

10. Children are more likely to be injured in day care centers than at home. _____

11. Children in high quality day care programs tend to be healthier than those not in day care. _____

12. Children in the United States are less likely to be poor than in other major industrialized countries. _____

13. Homelessness is closely related to low birth weight. _____

14. There is no treatment for lead poisoning. _____

15. Most cases of maltreatment of children involve physical abuse. _____

16. Most child abusers have psychotic or malicious personalities. _____

17. A abusive mother is likely to be impulsive or apathetic. _____

18. Low-income urban neighborhoods have almost uniformly high rates of child abuse. _____

19. Cultural approval of spanking as punishment may be related to the incidence of child abuse. _____

20. Children who are sexually abused are likely to be sexually maladjusted as adults. _____

# ANSWER KEY FOR CHAPTER 9

## CHAPTER 9 REVIEW

### Important Terms for Section I
1. transitional
2. urination

### Important Terms for Section II
1. gross motor
2. fine motor
3. action
4. preference

### Important Terms for Section IV
1. body
2. battered child
3. neglect
4. older
5. nonphysical
6. failure

## CHAPTER 9 QUIZ

### Matching--Numbers
1. e
2. a
3. d
4. h
5. i
6. g
7. j
8. f
9. b
10. c

### Multiple-Choice
1. a
2. c
3. b
4. a
5. d
6. b
7. c
8. c
9. c
10. b
11. d
12. b
13. c
14. d
15. c
16. c
17. b
18. d
19. c
20. a

### True or False?
1. T
2. F-To prevent damage, thumb-sucking should be stopped well before the permanent teeth come in.
3. T
4. T
5. F-Five-year-old girls are better at catching balls and other tasks involving small muscle coordination.
6. T
7. F-Kellogg recommends that adults let children draw what they like without imposing suggestions; pressure to portray reality leads children to move away from a concern with form and design.
8. F-In early childhood the lungs are not yet fully developed.
9. T- In the U.S.
10. F-Children suffer fewer injuries in day care centers than at home.
11. T
12. F-Child poverty rates in the U.S. are 1½ to 8 times as high as in other major industrialized countries.
13. T
14. F-Moderate lead poisoning can be treated.
15. F-About half of all cases of maltreatment involve neglect; one-fourth involve physical abuse.
16. F-More than 90 percent of child abusers are not psychotic; and far from being malicious, they often hate themselves for what they do but cannot control themselves.
17. T
18. F-Child abuse rates in low-income neighborhoods vary greatly, depending on such factors as community programs and social support.
19. T
20. T

## OVERVIEW

Chapter 10 focuses on the rapid development of cognitive skills during the preschool years. In this chapter, the authors:

❑ Explore advances and limitations in preschool children's thinking

❑ Report research showing that young children are more cognitively competent than Piaget believed

❑ Trace the development of language and memory in early childhood

❑ Discuss two approaches to the assessment of intelligence in early childhood

❑ Examine factors that influence the development of cognitive abilities

❑ Discuss goals, trends, and issues in early childhood education

## GUIDEPOSTS FOR STUDY

10.1 What are typical cognitive advances and immature aspects of preschool children's thinking?

10.2 How does language improve, and what happens when its development is delayed?

10.3 What memory abilities expand in early childhood?

10.4 How is preschoolers' intelligence measured and what factors influence it?

10.5 What purposes does early childhood education serve and how do children make the transition to kindergarten?

## CHAPTER 10 REVIEW

### Section I Piagetian Approach: The Preoperational Child

FRAMEWORK FOR SECTION I

A.      Advances in Preoperational Thought

1.   The Symbolic Function

2.   Early Symbolic Development and Spatial Thinking

3.   Causality

4.   Understanding of Identities and Categorization

5.   Number

B.      Immature Aspects of Preoperational Thought

1.   Conservation

2.   Egocentrism

C.      Do Young Children Have Theories of Mind?

1.   Knowledge about Thinking

2.   Social Cognition

3.   False Beliefs and Deception

4.   Distinguishing between Appearance and Reality

5.   Distinguishing between Fantasy and Reality

6. Influences on Theory-of-Mind Development

## IMPORTANT TERMS FOR SECTION I

**Completion:** Fill in the blanks to complete the definitions of key terms for this section of Chapter 10.

1. **preoperational stage:** In Piaget's theory, the second major stage of cognitive development (approximately from age 2 to age 7), in which children become more sophisticated in their use of _____ thought but are not yet able to use _____

2. _____ _____: In Piaget's terminology, ability to use mental representations (words, numbers, or images) to which a child has attached meaning.

3. _____: In Piaget's terminology, a limitation of preoperational thought that leads the child to focus on one aspect of a situation and neglect others, often leading to illogical conclusions.

4. _____: In Piaget's terminology, to think simultaneously about several aspects of a situation; characteristic of operational thought.

5. **conservation:** In Piaget's terminology, awareness that two objects that are equal according to a certain measure (such as length, weight, or quantity) remain equal in the face of _____ alteration (for example, a change in shape) so long as nothing has been added to or taken away from either object.

6. _____: In Piaget's terminology, a limitation on preoperational thinking consisting of failure to understand that an operation can go in two or more directions.

7. **transduction:** In Piaget's terminology, a preoperational child's tendency to mentally link particular experiences, whether or not there is logically a _____ relationship.

8. _____: In Piaget's terminology, inability to consider another person's point of view; a characteristic of preoperational thought.

9. **animism:** Tendency to attribute _____ to objects that are not _____.

10. _____: Ability to put oneself in another person's place and feel what that person feels.

11. **theory of mind:** Awareness and understanding of mental _____

## LEARNING OBJECTIVES FOR SECTION I

After reading and reviewing this section of Chapter 10, you should be able to do the following.

1. Tell what Piaget observed to be the chief difference between children's cognitive abilities in early childhood and middle childhood.

2. Name five cognitive advances of the preoperational stage and explain their significance.

3. Name three ways in which young children display the symbolic function, and give an example of each.

4. Give an example of each of the following achievements: understanding of identities, understanding of cause and effect, and ability to classify.

5. List five principles of counting that children recognize by early childhood.

6. Give examples of each of the following limitations Piaget observed in preoperational thought: centration, irreversibility, focus on states rather than on transformations, transductive reasoning, and egocentrism.

7. Identify and describe seven types of conservation and give an example of each.

8. Explain why Piaget may have underestimated children's thought processes, and discuss research on egocentrism, animism, and empathy which challenges his conclusions.

9. Discuss four aspects of young children's theory of mind, according to current research.

10. Tell under what circumstances cognitive abilities can be accelerated through training.

## Section II Language Development

## FRAMEWORK FOR SECTION II

A.      Vocabulary
B.      Grammar and Syntax
C.      Pragmatics and Social Speech
D.      Private Speech
E.      Delayed Language Development
F.      Social Interaction and Preparation for Literacy

## IMPORTANT TERMS FOR SECTION II

**Completion:** Fill in the blanks to complete the definitions of key terms for this section of Chapter 10.

1. _____ _____: Process by which a child absorbs the meaning of a new word after hearing it only once or twice in conversation.
2. **pragmatics:** The practical knowledge needed to use language for _____ purposes.
3. _____ **speech:** Speech intended to be understood by a listener.
4. _____ **speech:** Talking aloud to oneself with no intent to communicate.

## LEARNING OBJECTIVES FOR SECTION II

After reading and reviewing this section of Chapter 10, you should be able to do the following.

1. Identify advances in vocabulary, grammar, and syntax during early childhood, and name four limitations on young children's use of language.

2. Identify advances in young children's ability to communicate through speech.

3. List seven types of private speech, and give an example of each type.

4. Compare two views of the function and value of private speech, tell which view seems to be supported by research, and point out practical implications.

5. Discuss causes, implications, and treatment of delayed language development.

6. Identify three factors that can foster the development of literacy.

7. Discuss how parents foster young children's narrative skills.

**Section III Information-Processing Approach: Memory Development**

FRAMEWORK FOR SECTION III

A.     Recognition and Recall

B.     Forming Childhood Memories

D.     Influences on Autobiographical Memory

E.     Implicit Memory

IMPORTANT TERMS FOR SECTION III

**Completion:** Fill in the blank to complete the definition of the key term for this section of Chapter 10.

1. **recognition:** Ability to identify a _____ encountered stimulus. Compare <u>recall.</u>

2. **recall:** Ability to reproduce material from _____. Compare recognition.
3. _____ **memory:** Memory that produces a script of familiar routines to guide behavior.
4. **script:** General remembered outline of a familiar, _____ event, used to guide behavior.
5. _____ **memory:** Long-term memory of specific experiences or events, linked to time and place.
6. _____ **memory:** Memory of specific events in one's own life.

## LEARNING OBJECTIVES FOR SECTION III

After reading and reviewing this section of Chapter 10, you should be able to do the following.

1. Distinguish between recognition and recall, tell which is more difficult for young children, and name two factors influencing how well young children recall.

2. Explain the difference between implicit and explicit memory, and tell how it helps explain infantile amnesia.

3. Distinguish among generic memory, episodic memory, and autobiographical memory, and discuss the possibility of a link between autobiographical memory and language.

4. Identify and discuss factors that influence young children's ability to remember an event.

**Section IV Intelligence: Psychometric and Vygotskian Approaches**

## FRAMEWORK FOR SECTION IV

A.      Traditional Psychometric Measures

B.      Influences on Measured Intelligence
      1.   Temperament and Parent-Child Interaction

      2.   The Family Environment

C.      Testing and Teaching Based on Vygotsky's Theory


## IMPORTANT TERMS FOR SECTION IV

**Completion:** Fill in the blank to complete the definition of the key term for this section of Chapter 10.

  1.  **Stanford-Binet Intelligence Scale:** Individual intelligence test used with children to measure memory, _____ orientation, and practical judgment.

  2.  **Wechsler Preschool and Primary Scale of Intelligence--Revised (WPPSI-R):** Individual childhood intelligence test for children ages 3 to 7, which yields verbal and _____ scores as well as a combined score.


## LEARNING OBJECTIVES FOR SECTION IV

After reading and reviewing this section of Chapter 10, you should be able to do the following.

  1.  Explain why psychometric tests are more reliable for preschoolers than for infants.

  2.  Name and describe two psychometric intelligence tests used with young children.

3. List several factors that influence children's performance on intelligence tests.

4. Assess the impact of musical training on spatial reasoning.

5. Explain the relationships between socioeconomic status and other factors than can influence IQ.

6. Explain how Vygotsky's concepts of the zone of proximal development and scaffolding can be used to assess and develop young children's cognitive potential.

**Section V Early Childhood Education**

FRAMEWORK FOR SECTION V

A.      Goals and Types of Preschools: A Cross-Cultural View

B.      Compensatory Preschool Programs

C.      The Transition to Kindergarten

LEARNING OBJECTIVES FOR SECTION V

After reading and reviewing this section of Chapter 10, you should be able to do the following.

1. Give examples of cultural differences in goals for, and methods of, preschool education in the United States, Japan, and China.

2. Tell at least two ways in which a good preschool can foster children's development.

3. State the goals of compensatory preschool programs, and assess the short-term and long-term benefits of Project Head Start and other compensatory programs.

4. Summarize research on the value and long-term effects of an academic emphasis in preschool and kindergarten.

5. Give pros and cons of full-day kindergarten.

6. Name at least two predictors of future school achievement that can be observed in kindergarten.

7. Assess the long-term effects of delayed school entrance.

## CHAPTER 10 QUIZ

**Matching**--Terms and Situations: Match each of the situations described in the left-hand column with the applicable term in the right-hand column.

1. Andy saw his parents leave for the hospital and saw them bring his baby brother home for the first time. He thinks that they went to the hospital and picked out a baby. _____

2. Scott puts on a lion costume for Halloween. His baby sister cries when she sees him. "Don't worry; I'm still Scott," he says. _____

3. Amy is sitting in the back seat of the family car; she is wearing sandals. Her father is driving. "Look, Daddy," says Amy, "I have a sore on my toe." Her father replies, "I can't see it right now-I'll look at it later." "Why can't you see it?" asks Amy. _____

4. Ann and her older sister Maria are having lunch. Their mother pours a mug of soup for each. Although the two portions are equal, Maria's mug is taller and narrower than Ann's. "She got more," Ann complains. "Hers is bigger." _____

5. Charles wore his raincoat to preschool one day. It rained. The next day he refused to wear his raincoat. "I don't want it to rain," he explained. _____

6. Rita sees her mother working at a computer. The next day, while playing "office," she "types" on a toy typewriter. _____

7. On Mother's Day, Emmett picks a flower and gives it to a neighbor woman. "Why did you do that?" asks his mother. "Because she doesn't have any children," he replies. _____

a. deferred imitation

b. understanding of identities

c. empathy

d. egocentrism

e. conservation

f. focus on states rather than transformation

g. transduction

**Multiple-Choice:** Circle the choice that best completes or answers each item.

1. The symbolic function is characterized by
   a. sensory cues
   b. mental representations
   c. abstract thinking
   d. all of the above

2. <u>All but which</u> of the following are manifestations of the symbolic function?
   a. language
   b. deferred imitation
   c. invisible imitation
   d. symbolic play

3. Ten beads are arranged in a row. Whether they are counted from left to right or from right to left, there are 10 beads. This is an example of which principle?
   a. 1-to-1
   b. stable-order
   c. order-irrelevance
   d. cardinality

4. According to Piaget, children at the preoperational stage tend to
   a. conserve
   b. decenter
   c. centrate
   d. focus on transformations rather than states

5. <u>All but which</u> of the following are limitations of preoperational thought identified by Piaget?
   a. egocentrism
   b. animism
   c. irreversibility
   d. induction

6. Research indicates that Piaget underestimated preoperational children's ability to
   a. distinguish between appearance and reality
   b. distinguish between real and imagined events
   c. both a and b
   d. neither a nor b

7. Ten beads are arranged in a circle. If they are rearranged in a row, they will be the same 10 beads. This is an example of the principle of
   a. identity
   b. reversibility
   c. compensation
   d. abstraction

8. Overregularization of linguistic rules is a sign of
   a. development of social speech
   b. too much correction by adults
   c. linguistic progress
   d. an academic preschool background

9. Children begin to develop the ability to converse at about age
   a. 2
   b. 3
   c. 4
   d. 5

10. Which of the following viewed private speech as a sign of cognitive immaturity?
   a. Watson
   b. Piaget
   c. Vygotsky
   d. Kohlberg

11. Children with delayed language development
   a. have below-average intelligence
   b. come from homes where they do not get enough linguistic input
   c. have parents who use complex speech with them
   d. may need to hear a word more often than other children to learn its meaning

12. To best encourage young children's language development, adults should
   a. engage in simple conversations with them, using common words
   b. talk about personal topics, food, and table manners
   c. talk about things the adults are interested in
   d. encourage imaginative play

13. Children develop better narrative skills when parents do <u>all but which</u> of the following?
   a. talk with them about past events
   b. prompt them with contextual cues
   c. take the lead in conversations
   d. comment on children's feelings about events

14. Research suggests that the most important factor in young children's ability to recall is
   a. general knowledge
   b. memory strategies
   c. mastery motivation
   d. intelligence

15. Memory without awareness is called
    a. implicit
    b. explicit
    c. generic
    d. none of the above; memory is not possible without awareness
16. Episodic memories
    a. rarely become part of autobiographical memory
    b. are long-lasting even in 2-year-olds
    c. are better retained by boys than by girls
    d. are best retained when talked about
17. Young children best remember things they
    a. see
    b. do for the first time
    c. have done once or twice before
    d. do frequently
18. The revised version of the Stanford-Binet Intelligence Scale, prepared in 1985, primarily emphasizes
    a. IQ as an overall measure of intelligence
    b. verbal items
    c. nonverbal items
    d. patterns and levels of cognitive development
19. Which of the following statements about performance on intelligence tests is true?
    a. Because intelligence is inborn, an individual's IQ is fairly stable; thus test performance, in general, has remained approximately constant.
    b. Experience and other factors can contribute to a rise or fall in IQ; but, on the average, test performance has remained approximately constant.
    c. Experience and other factors can contribute to a rise or fall in IQ; test performance, in general, has improved in recent years.
    d. Experience and other factors can contribute to a rise or fall in IQ; test performance, in general, has declined in recent years.
20. Which of the following appears to be true of the relationship between socioeconomic status and a child's IQ?
    a. Socioeconomic status is the most important factor in IQ.
    b. Socioeconomic status is the least important factor in IQ.
    c. Socioeconomic status bears little relationship to IQ.
    d. Socioeconomic status is one of several social and family risk factors that affect IQ.
21. The zone of proximal development is the level at which children can
    a. perform a task easily on their own
    b. perform a task on their own, but with difficulty
    c. perform a task with some guidance
    d. not perform a task at all
22. In which country is academic instruction in preschool most highly valued?
    a. China
    b. United States
    c. Japan
    d. All of the above place an equally high value on academic instruction.
23. Students from deprived backgrounds who participated in Project Head Start are more likely than youngsters from similar backgrounds who did not participate to
    a. show lasting gains in IQ
    b. finish high school
    c. do as well in school as average middle-class children
    d. none of the above; the program has had no measurable long-term effects
24. Children in academically oriented preschool programs
    a. recognize numbers better than children in child-centered programs
    b. take more pride in their accomplishments
    c. are more highly motivated
    d. are more dependent on adult approval

**True or False?** In the blank following each item, write T (for true) or F (for false). In the space below each item, if the statement is false, rewrite it to make it true.

1. Symbolic thought depends on sensory cues. _____

2. It is common for a 6-year-old to believe that growth since infancy has made him or her a different person. _____

3. Not until age 7 or 8 can children classify items using two criteria. _____

4. According to Piaget, children at the preoperational stage do not understand that water poured from a pitcher into a glass can be restored to its original state by pouring it back into the pitcher. _____

5. Egocentrism, for Piaget, means selfishness. _____

6. Preschool children realize that thought is continuous. _____

7. Research suggests that 3-year-olds tend to confuse appearance with reality. _____

8. When a child is on the verge of grasping a new concept, training may accelerate that process. _____

9. Children ages 4 to 5 can use prepositions. _____

10. Research has confirmed Piaget's view that most preschool speech is egocentric. _____

11. The most sociable children tend to use private speech the most. _____

147

12. A preschooler with delayed language development is likely to be unpopular. _____

13. A young child recalls paired items better when they belong to the same category (for example, a car and an airplane) than when one is a part of the other (for example, a wheel and a car). _____

14. Autobiographical memory typically begins before 3 years of age. _____

15. In court cases concerning charges of child abuse, preschoolers tend to be less reliable witnesses than older children. _____

16. The Stanford-Binet Intelligence Scale and the Wechsler Preschool and Primary Scale of Intelligence--Revised (WPPSI-R) are group tests often administered in early childhood. _____

17. The more assistance and approval mothers give 2½-year-olds in solving problems, the better the children do on intelligence tests at age 5. _____

18. Children whose parents help them with a task they haven't quite mastered tend to become overly dependent on parental support. _____

19. Project Head Start is a compensatory preschool program for poor minority children. _____

20. The neediest children in Project Head Start make the greatest short-term cognitive gains. _____

21. Children who attend academically oriented preschools tend to excel throughout their school careers. _____

22. The most important behavioral predictor of future school achievement is attentiveness_____

# ANSWER KEY FOR CHAPTER 10

## CHAPTER 10 REVIEW

### Important Terms for Section I
1. symbolic, logic
2. symbolic function
3. centration
4. decenter
5. perceptual
6. irreversibility
7. causal
8. egocentrism
9. life, alive
10. empathy
11. processes

### Important Terms for Section II
1. fast mapping
2. communicative
3. social
4. private

### Important Terms for Section III
1. previously
2. memory
3. generic
4. repeated
5. episodic
6. autobiographical

### Important Terms for Section IV
1. spatial
2. performance

## CHAPTER 10 QUIZ

### Matching--Terms and Situations
1. f
2. b
3. d
4. e
5. g
6. a
7. c

### Multiple-Choice
1. b
2. c
3. c
4. c
5. d
6. b
7. a
8. c
9. a
10. b
11. d
12. d
13. c
14. c
15. a
16. d
17. b
18. d
19. c
20. d
21. c
22. a
23. b
24. d

### True or False?
1. F-Symbolic thought is independent of sensory cues.
2. F-During the preoperational stage, children develop an understanding of identity.
3. F-Many 4-year-olds can classify by two criteria.
4. T
5. F-Egocentrism is not selfishness but self-centered understanding, according to Piaget.
6. F-Preschool children seem to believe that thought starts and stops.
7. T
8. T
9. T
10. F-Recent research shows that children's speech is quite social from an early age.
11. T
12. T
13. F-A young child recalls paired items better when one is a part of the other.
14. F-Autobiographical memory typically begins around age 4 and rarely before age 3.
15. T
16. F-The Stanford-Binet and the Wechsler are individual tests.
17. F-Children whose mothers give much assistance or approval may not develop independent problem-solving skills; children whose mothers suggest effective strategies do better.

18. F-Scaffolding, or temporary support, can help children master a task; the more finely tuned the help, the better a child does.
19. F-Project Head Start is for low-income children, regardless of race or ethnic origin.
20. T
21. F-Children who attend academically oriented preschools may excel during the early years of school but tend to lose their advantage later.
22. T

# CHAPTER 11
# PSYCHOSOCIAL DEVELOPMENT IN EARLY CHILDHOOD

## OVERVIEW

Chapter 11 traces several strands of psychosocial development in early childhood. In this chapter, the authors:

❑ Trace the development of young children's sense of self, understanding of emotions, and self-esteem

❑ Present Erikson's "crisis" of early childhood, initiative versus guilt.

❑ Discuss how children develop gender identity, and explore theories and research on how gender differences come about

❑ Describe types of play, and examine how culture influences play

❑ Assess the influence of child-rearing styles and practices

❑ Explain how altruism (prosocial behavior), aggression, and fearfulness develop, and how they are influenced by parental treatment

❑ Describe relationships with siblings and peers, characteristics of the only child, and how family relationships and peer relationships influence each other

## GUIDEPOSTS FOR STUDY

11.1 How does the self-concept develop during early childhood and how do children advance in understanding their emotions?

11.2 How do young children develop initiative and self-esteem?

11.3 How do boys and girls become aware of the meaning of gender and what are four theoretical explanations for differences in behavior between the sexes?

11.4 How do preschoolers play and how does play contribute to and reflect development?

11.5 What three main forms of discipline and four parenting styles do parents use and how do parenting practices affect development?

11.6 Why do young children help or hurt others and why do they develop fears?

11.7 How do young children get along with (or without) siblings?

11.8 How do young children choose playmates and friends and why are some children more popular than others?

## CHAPTER 11 REVIEW

### Section I   The Developing Self

FRAMEWORK FOR SECTION I

A.     The Self-Concept and Cognitive Development
  1.   Early Self-Concept Development: The Continuous Self
  2.   Self-Definition: A Neo-Piagetian View

B.     Understanding Emotions
  1.   Emotions Directed Toward the Self
  2.   Simultaneous Emotions

C.     Erikson: Initiative Versus Guilt

D.      Self-Esteem

## IMPORTANT TERMS FOR SECTION I

**Completion:** Fill in the blanks to complete the definitions of key terms for this section of Chapter 11.

1.  **self-_____:** Sense of self; descriptive and evaluative mental picture of one's abilities and traits.
2.  **self- _____:** Cluster of characteristics used to describe oneself.
3.  **single _____:** In neo-Piagetian terminology, first stage in development of self-definition, in which children describe themselves in terms of individual, unconnected characteristics and in all-or-nothing terms.
4.  **real self:** The self one actually _____. Compare ideal self.
5.  **ideal self:** The self one would like to _____. Compare real self.
6.  **representational _____:** In neo-Piagetian terminology, the second stage in development of self-definition, in which a child makes logical connections between aspects of the self but still sees these characteristics in all-or-nothing terms.
7.  **_____ versus _____:** In Erikson's theory, the third crisis in psychosocial development, occurring between the ages of 3 and 6, in which children must balance the urge to pursue goals with the moral reservations that may prevent carrying them out.
8.  **self-_____:** The judgment a person makes about his or her self-worth.


## LEARNING OBJECTIVES FOR SECTION I

After reading and reviewing this section of Chapter 11, you should be able to do the following.

1.  Explain the shift in self-awareness that occurs around age 4.




2.  Describe two steps in self-definition that occur between ages 4 and 6, according to neo-Piagetian theory.




3.  Describe four levels of understanding of emotions directed toward the self that children typically undergo between ages 4 and 8.

4. Describe five levels of understanding of simultaneous emotions that children typically undergo between ages 4 and 12.

5. Identify the conflict involved in Erikson's third "crisis"--initiative versus guilt--and summarize the outcome of a successful or unsuccessful resolution of that crisis.

6. Explain how self-esteem in early childhood differs from self-esteem in middle childhood, and identify sources of self-esteem in early childhood.

7. Tell how the "helpless" pattern can arise, and what its consequences may be.

**Section II  Gender**

FRAMEWORK FOR SECTION II

A.  Gender Differences

B.  Perspectives on Gender Development: Nature and Nurture
   1.  Biological Approach
   2.  Psychoanalytic Approach
   3.  Cognitive Approach
   4.  Socialization-Based Approach

IMPORTANT TERMS FOR SECTION II

**Completion:**  Fill in the blanks to complete the definitions of key terms for this section of Chapter 11.

1. _____ _____: Awareness, developed in early childhood, that one is male or female.
2. _____ **differences:** Psychological or behavioral differences between males and females.
3. _____ _____: Behaviors, interests, attitudes, skills, and traits that a culture considers appropriate for males or for females.

4. _____ _____: Socialization process by which children, at an early age, learn behavior deemed appropriate by the culture for a boy or girl.
5. _____ _____: Exaggerated generalizations about male or female role behavior.
6. _____: In Freudian theory, the process by which a young child adopts characteristics, beliefs, attitudes, values, and behaviors of the parent of the same sex.
7. **gender** _____, or **sex-**_____ _____: Awareness that one will always be male or female.
8. **gender-**_____ **theory:** Theory, proposed by Bem, that children socialize themselves in their gender roles by developing a concept of what it means to be male or female in a particular culture.
9. **gender** _____: In Bem's theory, a pattern of behavior organized around gender.

## LEARNING OBJECTIVES FOR SECTION II

After reading and reviewing this section of Chapter 11, you should be able to do the following.

1. Assess the extent of physical, cognitive, and personality differences between boys and girls.

2. Explain the importance of gender roles and gender-typing and the danger of gender stereotypes.

3. Assess the evidence for biological influences on behavioral differences between males and females.

4. Discuss the influence of parents (especially fathers) on gender-typing.

5. Discuss the influences of television and children's books on gender stereotypes.

**Section III  Play: The Business of Early Childhood**

## FRAMEWORK FOR SECTION III

A.  Types of Play

B.  The Social Dimension of Play

C.  How Gender Influences Play

D.  How Culture Influences Play

## IMPORTANT TERMS FOR SECTION III

Completion:  Fill in the blank to complete the definitions of the key terms for this section of Chapter 11.

1.  **social play:** Play in which children, to varying degrees, interact with other _____.

2.  _____ _____**play:** Forms of play that reveal children's mental development.

3.  _____**play:** Play involving imaginary people or situations; also called <u>fantasy play</u>, <u>dramatic play</u>, <u>symbolic play</u>, or <u>imaginative play.</u>

## LEARNING OBJECTIVES FOR SECTION III

After reading and reviewing this section of Chapter 11, you should be able to do the following.

1.  Name six types of social and nonsocial play identified by Mildred Parten; summarize research on the types of play that occur in day care centers, and on the value of nonsocial play.

2.  Name four types of cognitive play identified by Piaget, trace the development of pretend play, and explain its significance.

3.  Discuss how culture influences forms of play, and give an example.

**Section IV  Parenting**

## FRAMEWORK FOR SECTION IV

A.    Forms of Discipline
    1.  Reinforcement and Punishment
    2.  Power Assertion, Induction, and Withdrawal of Love

B.    Parenting Styles
    1.  Baumrind's Model
    2.  Support and Critics of Baumrind's Model
    3.  Cultural Differences in Parenting Styles

C.    Promoting Altruism and Dealing with Aggression and Fearfulness
    1.  Prosocial Behavior
    2.  Aggression
    3.  Fearfulness

## IMPORTANT TERMS FOR SECTION IV

Completion:  Fill in the blanks to complete the definitions of key terms for this section of Chapter 11.

1.  **discipline:** Tool for socialization, which includes methods of molding children's character and of teaching them to exercise self-_____ and engage in acceptable behavior.
2.  **authoritarian:** In Baumrind's terminology, parenting style emphasizing control and _____. Compare <u>authoritative</u> and <u>permissive.</u>
3.  **permissive:** In Baumrind's terminology, parenting style emphasizing self-_____ and self-regulation. Compare <u>authoritarian</u> and <u>authoritative.</u>
4.  **authoritative:** In Baumrind's terminology, parenting style blending respect for a child's _____ with an effort to instill social values. Compare <u>authoritarian</u> and <u>permissive.</u>
5.  **altruism, or prosocial behavior**  Behavior intended to help others without external _____.
6.  _____**aggression:** Aggressive behavior used as a means of achieving a goal.
7.  _____**aggression:** Aggressive behavior intended to hurt another person.

## LEARNING OBJECTIVES FOR SECTION IV

After reading and reviewing this section of Chapter 11, you should be able to do the following.

1.  Compare the effectiveness of reinforcement and punishment.

2.  Differentiate between internal and external rewards, giving an example of each.

3. Cite at least three dangers of harsh punishment, and list four factors that influence the effectiveness of punishment.

4. Compare power assertion, induction, and withdrawal of love, and discuss factors affecting the choice among these strategies.

5. Compare authoritarian, permissive, and authoritative styles of parenting as identified by Baumrind, and evaluate Baumrind's research.

6. Discuss how parents and preschool children negotiate and resolve conflicts, and how such negotiations can contribute to internalization and other goals of parenting.

7.  Compare the long-term effects of specific child-rearing practices with the effect of loving treatment.

8.  Identify factors in the child, the family, the school, and the culture that contribute to altruism, or prosocial behavior.

9.  Distinguish between instrumental and hostile aggression, and trace shifts in aggressive behavior in early childhood.

10. Identify factors that can trigger aggression.

11. Discuss sources of young children's fears and methods of prevention and treatment.

**Section V  Relationships with Other Children**

FRAMEWORK FOR SECTION V

A.      Siblings--or Their Absence
    1.   Brothers and Sisters
    2.   The Only Child

B.      Playmates and Friends
    1.   Choosing Playmates and Friends
    2.   Characteristics and Effects of Friendships
    3.   Parenting and Popularity
    4.   Helping Children with Peer Relations


LEARNING OBJECTIVES FOR SECTION V

After reading and reviewing this section of Chapter 11, you should be able to do the following.

1.  Describe typical sibling interactions in early childhood, and how siblings resolve disputes.

2.  Summarize research, especially in China, on characteristics of only children, and discuss implications of China's "one-child" policy.

3.  Give reasons for the tendency toward sex segregation in play among preschoolers.

4.  Identify important features of early friendships and behavior patterns that affect the choice of playmates and friends.

5. List several benefits of friendship during the preschool years.

6. Discuss ways in which behavior patterns in sibling relationships may carry over to peer relationships, and vice versa.

7. Discuss how parenting style and practices influence popularity, and suggest ways adults can help children find playmates and friends.

## CHAPTER 11 QUIZ

Matching--Who's Who:  Match each name in the left-hand column with the appropriate description from the right-hand column.

1. Susan Harter _____

2. Lawrence Kohlberg _____

3. Erik Erikson _____

4. Sandra Bem _____

5. Maccoby & Martin _____

6. Jean Piaget _____

7. Albert Bandura _____

8. Mildred B. Parten _____

9. Diana Baumrind _____

10. Sigmund Freud _____

a.  originated gender-schema theory

b.  parenting style of neglectful or uninvolved

c.  studied the self-concept and understanding of emotions

d.  identified styles of parenting

e.  described gender identity as the result of repression of the wish to possess the parent of the other sex and identification with the same-sex parent

f.  linked gender identity to gender constancy

g.  identified types of social and nonsocial play

h.  studied frustration and imitation as triggers for aggression

i.  identified categories of play linked to cognitive development

j.  theorized that children need to balance initiative and guilt

**Multiple-Choice:** Circle the choice that best completes or answers each item.

1. A shift in self-awareness that seems to occur around age 4 is
   a. the ability to recognize oneself in a mirror
   b. the ability to recognize oneself in a photograph
   c. the understanding that the self is continuous in time
   d. the ability to integrate features of the self into a general concept

2. According to neo-Piagetian thinkers, the ability to link two aspects of the self generally occurs at about age(s)
   a. 2 to 3
   b. 4
   c. 5 to 6
   d. 7

3. Unsuccessful resolution of the crisis of initiative versus guilt may cause
   a. impotence
   b. inhibition
   c. intolerance
   d. any of the above

4. Regarding self-esteem, 4- to 7-year-olds are different from older children in that
   a. younger children have not yet developed a sense of self-esteem
   b. older children have an all-or-nothing opinion of themselves
   c. preschool children cannot express their self-worth in words
   d. younger children underrate their abilities

5. Which of the following is not strongly correlated with self-esteem in early childhood?
   a. child's sense of own competence
   b. child's curiosity
   c. child's adaptability
   d. supportive feedback from adults

6. Gender differences are
   a. physical differences between males and females
   b. psychological or behavioral differences between males and females
   c. attitudes deemed appropriate for males and females
   d. all of the above

7. Research on gender differences has found that
   a. aside from anatomy, young boys and girls are more alike than different
   b. boys excel in computation and understanding of mathematical concepts
   c. girls have superior verbal ability from early childhood on
   d. boys have superior spatial ability from early childhood on

8. Gender roles include
   a. interests
   b. skills
   c. both a and b
   d. neither a nor b

9. All but which of the following statements seems to contradict social-learning theory's explanation for the acquisition of gender roles?
   a. Children do not always imitate adults of the same sex.
   b. Children are no more like their parents than they are like other randomly-chosen parents.
   c. Some gender-typed behavior may reflect the child's own preferences.
   d. Gender roles can be modified.

10. According to Kohlberg, gender identity is typically acquired at about age
    a. 2 to 3
    b. 4 to 5
    c. 6 to 7
    d. 8 to 9

11. According to Bem, parents can raise children without gender stereotypes by following all but which of the following suggestions?
    a. exposing children to nontraditional occupations
    b. giving them nonstereotyped gifts
    c. sharing household tasks
    d. deemphasizing anatomical differences

12. According to Bem, an androgynous personality is
    a. predominantly "masculine"
    b. predominantly "feminine"
    c. highly adaptable
    d. sexually repressed

13. According to Parten, which of the following shows the most advancement toward social play?
    a. building a block tower alongside another child who is building a block tower
    b. playing with a truck near other children who are building a block tower
    c. watching other children build a block tower
    d. talking to children who are building a block tower

14. According to research done since 1970, which of the following statements about preschool children's play is <u>not</u> true?
    a. Some children's play is more social than others'.
    b. Social play seems to have decreased since the 1920s.
    c. Parallel constructive play is common among socially skilled children.
    d. Solitary play is a sign of immaturity.

15. A 3-year-old pushing a toy train and saying "choo-choo" is engaged in what kind of play?
    a. functional
    b. pretend
    c. constructive
    d. associative

16. Which of the following statements about children's play is true?
    a. Children who watch a lot of television play more imaginatively than children who watch little television.
    b. About one-third of kindergartners' play is pretend play.
    c. Children in small day care centers with same-age grouping play more sociably than other children.
    d. Korean American children engage in more social play than Anglo American children.

17. Punishment is more effective when it
    a. is consistent
    b. is performed by a person the child is afraid of
    c. is accompanied by a detailed explanation
    d. all of the above

18. Inductive techniques of socialization include <u>all but which</u> of the following?
    a. setting limits
    b. reasoning with a child
    c. demonstrating logical consequences of behavior
    d. generalizing about children's behavior

19. Baumrind's research suggests that the most effective style of parenting is
    a. authoritarian
    b. permissive
    c. authoritative
    d. All of the above are equally effective.

20. The upbringing of Chinese children emphasizes <u>all but which</u> of the following?
    a. warmth and supportiveness
    b. obedience to elders
    c. self-reliance
    d. firm control

21. Preschoolers who won't let another child play near them are
    a. unsociable
    b. the least competent
    c. behaving normally
    d. likely to be aggressive at age 8

22. According to social-learning theory and research, <u>all but which</u> of the following statements about aggression in young children are true?
    a. A frustrated child is more likely to act aggressively than a contented one.
    b. Children who have seen an aggressive adult are more likely to act aggressively.
    c. Televised violence tends to promote aggression.
    d. Spanking is generally an effective way to curb aggression.

23. The most common fears of children ages 3 to 6 include <u>all but which</u> of the following?
    a. dogs
    b. thunderstorms
    c. death
    d. doctors

24. An effective way to help young children overcome fears is
    a. making light of their fears
    b. explaining why their fears are unreasonable
    c. encouraging expression of fears
    d. removing a feared object

25. Which of the following is more important to 4-year-olds than to 7-year-olds in choosing friends?
    a. physical characteristics
    b. affection
    c. support
    d. common activities

**True or False?** In the blank following each item, write T (for true) or F (for false). In the space below each item, if the statement is false, rewrite it to make it true.

1. A 4-year-old's self-definition focuses on observable, or external, aspects of the self. _____

2. Four-year-olds typically do not understand that they can have contradictory emotions at the same time. _____

3. Erikson's crisis of initiative versus guilt reflects a split between the childlike and adultlike parts of the personality. _____

4. Children with contingent self-esteem tend to show the "helpless" pattern of behavior. _____

5. Preschool boys show more spatial ability than preschool girls. _____

6. According to Freud, a girl becomes gender-typed through identification with her mother. _____

7. Research shows that children become gender-typed by imitating the same-sex parent. _____

8. Kohlberg suggested that gender constancy follows the establishment of gender differences in behavior. _____

9. Gender-schema theory holds that gender-typing can be deliberately modified. _____

10. Studies suggest that biological influences are the chief factor in gender differences. _____

# ANSWER KEY FOR CHAPTER 11

## CHAPTER 11 REVIEW

### Important Terms for Section I
1. concept
2. definition
3. representations
4. is
5. be
6. mappings
7. initiative, guilt
8. esteem

### Important Terms for Section II
1. gender identity
2. gender
3. gender roles
4. gender-typing
5. gender stereotypes
6. identification
7. constancy, category constancy
8. schema
9. schema

### Important Terms for Section III
1. children
2. cognitive levels of
3. pretend

### Important Terms for Section IV
1. control
2. obedience
3. expression
4. individuality
5. reward
6. instrumental
7. hostile

## CHAPTER 11 QUIZ

### Matching--Who's Who
1. c
2. f
3. j
4. a
5. b
6. i
7. h
8. g
9. d
10. e

### Multiple-Choice
1. c
2. c
3. d
4. c
5. a
6. b
7. a
8. c
9. d
10. a
11. d
12. c
13. a
14. d
15. b
16. b
17. a
18. d
19. d
20. c
21. c
22. d
23. c
24. c
25. a

### True or False?
1. T
2. T
3. T
4. T
5. T
6. F-Children tend to be no more like their parents in personality than like a random set of parents, and no more like the same-sex parent than like the other parent.
7. F.
8. T-Kohlberg suggested that gender constancy precedes gender differences
9. F
10. T-Studies are inconclusive but suggest that both biology and environment play a role

# CHAPTER 12
## PHYSICAL DEVELOPMENT AND HEALTH IN MIDDLE CHILDHOOD

## OVERVIEW

Chapter 12 follows a child's physical growth and development during the elementary school years. In this chapter, the authors:

- ❑ Point out factors that influence height and weight and variations in growth in middle childhood
- ❑ Outline nutritional requirements and discuss their relationship to physiological and cognitive growth and development
- ❑ Discuss childhood obesity and body image
- ❑ Describe gender differences in motor skills, and discuss the role of organized sports and rough-and-tumble play
- ❑ Identify health and safety concerns and present recommendations for improving children's health and fitness
- ❑ Discuss how children's understanding of health and illness develops and how cultural attitudes affect health care

## GUIDEPOSTS FOR STUDY

12.1  What are normal growth patterns during middle childhood and how can abnormal growth be treated?

12.2  What are some nutritional and oral health concerns for school-age children?

12.3  What gains in motor skills typically occur at this age, and what kinds of play do boys and girls engage in?

12.4  What are the principal health and fitness concerns in middle childhood and what can adults do to make the school years healthier and safer?

## CHAPTER 12 REVIEW

### Section I Growth and Physical Development

FRAMEWORK FOR SECTION I

A.    Height and Weight
B.    Nutrition and Oral Health
1.    Tooth Development and Dental Care
2.    Malnutrition
C.    Obesity and Body Image
1.    Causes of Obesity
2.    Why Treat Childhood Obesity?
3.    Body Image and Eating Disorders

IMPORTANT TERM FOR SECTION I

**Completion:** Fill in the blank to complete the definition of the key term for this section of Chapter 12.

1. **body** _____: Descriptive and evaluative beliefs about one's appearance.

# LEARNING OBJECTIVES FOR SECTION I

After reading and reviewing this section of Chapter 12, you should be able to do the following.

1. Summarize the growth patterns of boys and girls in middle childhood and their average changes in height and weight.

2. Identify factors that may help account for ethnic variations in growth.

3. State considerations in treating children who are unusually short.

4. Outline nutritional needs during middle childhood.

5. Estimate the extent of malnutrition among children worldwide, and describe its cognitive and psychosocial effects and the effectiveness of interventions.

6. Assess the current state of dental health and dental care among school-age children, and suggest a way to deal with children's fear of going to the dentist.

7. Identify trends in the prevalence of obesity, discuss four possible causes of this condition, and evaluate various treatments.

8. Assess influences on children's concern with body image.

## Section II Motor Development and Physical Play
### FRAMEWORK FOR SECTION II
A.      Rough-and-Tumble Play

B.      Organized Sports

## IMPORTANT TERM FOR SECTION II
**Completion:** Fill in the blank to complete the definition of the key term for this section of Chapter 12.

1. _____-and-_____ **play:** Vigorous play involving wrestling, hitting, and chasing, often accompanied by laughing and screaming.

## LEARNING OBJECTIVES FOR SECTION II
After reading and reviewing this section of Chapter 12, you should be able to do the following.

1. Assess the roles of rough-and-tumble play and organized sports in school children's development.

2. Discuss factors contributing to gender differences in motor skills during middle childhood.

**Section III Health and Safety**

## FRAMEWORK FOR SECTION III

A.     Maintaining Health and Fitness

B.     Medical Problems

    1.   Vision and Hearing Problems

    2.   Stuttering

    3.   Asthma

    4.   HIV and AIDS

C.     Accidental Injuries


## IMPORTANT TERMS FOR SECTION III

**Completion:** Fill in the blanks to complete the definitions of key terms for this section of Chapter 12.

1.   **acute medical conditions:** Illnesses that last a _____ time.
2.   **chronic medical conditions:** Illnesses or impairments that persist for at least _____ _____.
3.   **stuttering:** Involuntary, frequent _____ or prolongation of sounds or syllables.
4.   **asthma:** A chronic respiratory disease characterized by sudden attacks of coughing, wheezing, and difficulty in _____.


## LEARNING OBJECTIVES FOR SECTION III

After reading and reviewing this section of Chapter 12, you should be able to do the following.

1.   Explain why today's schoolchildren are less fit than they should be and what can be done to improve their health and fitness.




2.   Describe cognitive changes in children's understanding of health and illness, and specifically of causes of AIDS, and describe research testing Piaget's theory on this point.




3.   Summarize the prevalence of various acute and chronic medical conditions in middle childhood, and tell how a chronic condition can affect everyday life.

4. Identify cultural factors in explanations for illness, and tell how cultural attitudes can affect health care.

5. Summarize causes and treatments for stuttering.

6. Describe normal changes in vision in middle childhood and summarize the incidence of vision and hearing problems.

7. Explain the relationship between the impact of asthma and access to health care.

8. Tell why accidental injury is a great concern in middle childhood; point out which children are at the greatest risk and where, and how accidents can be prevented.

# CHAPTER 12 QUIZ

**Matching--Numbers:** Match each of the items in the left-hand column with the correct number in the right-hand column.

1. Height (in inches) of average 9-year-old boy or girl _____

a.  6

2. Average number of calories (in hundreds) needed daily in middle childhood _____

b.  7

3. Age at which first molars typically erupt _____

c.  8

4. Age at which second molars typically erupt _____

d.  10

5. Percentile of weight-for-height indicating obesity _____

e.  11

6. Percentile of weight-for-height indicating obesity in 1973 _____

f.  13

7. Approximate percentage of U.S. children ages 6 to 17 who are obese _____

g.  24

8. Age at which typical child can balance on one foot without looking _____

h.  53

9. Age at which typical child can grip with 12 pounds of pressure _____

i.  85

10. Approximate percentage of prepubertal children who stutter _____

j.  95

**Multiple-Choice:** Circle the choice that best completes or answers each item.

1. The average annual weight gain (in pounds) in middle childhood is
   a.  1 to 2
   b.  3 to 4
   c.  5 to 8
   d.  9 to 12

2. Boys generally begin their growth spurt at about age
   a.  9
   b.  10 to 11
   c.  12 to 13
   d.  14

3. Which of the following statements about physical development and health in middle childhood is not true?
   a.  Girls retain more fatty tissue than boys.
   b.  Risk of accidental injury decreases.
   c.  Colds and sore throats are prevalent.
   d.  Motor abilities improve.

4. Eight-year-olds tend to be tallest in which of the following parts of the world?
   a.  southeast Asia
   b.  Oceania
   c.  South America
   d.  eastern Australia

5. Synthetic growth-hormone therapy has all but which of the following drawbacks?
   a.  side effects
   b.  uncertainty about safety
   c.  uncertainty about long-term effects
   d.  possibility of harming self-concept

6. Malnourished children tend to be all but which of the following?
   a.  stunted in growth
   b.  inattentive
   c.  hyperactive
   d.  anxious

7. The improvement in U.S. schoolchildren's dental health can be attributed largely to
   a. adhesive sealants
   b. less fear of the dentist than in early childhood
   c. fluoridated drinking water and toothpaste
   d. all of the above

8. All but which of the following have been advanced as possible causes of obesity?
   a. genetic predisposition
   b. late weaning during infancy
   c. watching television frequently
   d. being in a low socioeconomic group

9. Rough-and-tumble play
   a. represents at least 25 percent of schoolchildren's free play
   b. serves social as well as physical purposes
   c. occurs mainly in societies that emphasize fighting and hunting
   d. is more typical among older children than younger ones

10. Motor skills in which the greatest differences between prepubescent boys and girls appear are those which
   a. require support of body weight
   b. require eye-hand coordination
   c. reflect socioeconomic background
   d. depend on physical measurements

11. About what percentage of U.S. youth ages 8 to 16 fail to meet standards for cardiovascular fitness?
   a. 5
   b. 10 to 15
   c. 20
   d. 40

12. According to Piaget, a child who believes that diseases are caused by all-powerful germs is probably about how old?
   a. 2 to 3
   b. 4 to 6
   c. 7 to 10
   d. 11 to 13

13. Which child is least likely to have a visual problem or hearing loss?
   a. white
   b. African American
   c. Latino
   d. none of the above; no significant differences among these groups have been reported

14. Which child is most likely to have AIDS?
   a. white
   b. African American
   c. Hispanic
   d. none of the above; no significant differences among these groups have been reported

15. According to an American Academy of Pediatrics task force, a child who carries the HIV virus but does not show symptoms
   a. is likely to show developmental delays
   b. is likely to have behavior problems
   c. should be isolated to protect other children
   d. should have no special treatment

16. The leading cause of disability and death in children over 1 year of age is
   a. heart disease
   b. obesity
   c. accidental injury
   d. viral infection

17. Most childhood accidents occur
   a. in (or are inflicted by) automobiles or in the home
   b. in and around schools
   c. in team or individual sports
   d. at playgrounds

**True or False?** In the blank following each item, write T (for true) or F (for false). In the space below each item, if the statement is false, rewrite it to make it true.

1. White children are usually bigger than African American children of the same age and sex.

   _____

2. Very short children tend to be maladjusted. _____

171

3. Sugar makes children hyperactive. _____

4. Effects of malnutrition are untreatable. _____

5. Tooth decay can be prevented by the use of adhesive sealants on chewing surfaces. _____

6. Obesity is more common in the United States than during the early 1970s. _____

7. Behavioral modification has been somewhat effective in treating obesity. _____

8. Competitive team sports promote fitness in school-age children. _____

9. Blood pressure should be measured every year starting at age 3. _____

10. Most children with chronic medical conditions have problems in school. _____

11. Stuttering is more common in girls than in boys. _____

12. Children under 6 years old tend to be nearsighted. _____

13. Asthma can be fatal. _____

14. Children with AIDS often have developmental problems. _____

15. Boys at all ages have higher accident rates than girls. _____

16. Children with siblings are more likely to be injured than children who have no siblings. _____

# ANSWER KEY FOR CHAPTER 12

## CHAPTER 12 REVIEW

### Important Term for Section I
1. image

### Important Term for Section II
1. rough, tumble

### Important Terms for Section III
1. short
2. 3 months
3. repetition
4. breathing

## CHAPTER 12 QUIZ

### Matching--Numbers
1. h
2. g
3. a
4. f
5. j
6. i
7. e
8. b
9. c
10. d

### Multiple-Choice
1. c
2. c
3. b
4. d
5. a
6. c
7. c
8. b
9. b
10. a
11. c
12. c
13. b
14. b
15. d
16. c
17. a

### True or False?
1. F-African American children are usually somewhat taller and heavier than white children of the same age and sex.
2. F-Shortness in itself does not necessarily lead to serious adjustment problems.
3. F-Recent research suggests that sugar does not adversely affect children's behavior, cognitive functioning, or mood.
4. F-Interventions that include cognitive stimulation and formal schooling can at least partially offset poor outcomes of malnutrition.
5. T
6. T
7. T
8. F-Competitive team sports do not promote fitness but are engaged in by the children who already are most fit.
9. T
10. F-Most children with chronic conditions do not have problems in school.
11. F-Stuttering is 3 times more common in boys than in girls.
12. F-Children under 6 tend to be farsighted.
13. T
14. T
15. F-Boys have higher accident rates than girls except at age 1.
16. T

# CHAPTER 13
# COGNITIVE DEVELOPMENT IN MIDDLE CHILDHOOD

## OVERVIEW

Chapter 13 focuses on a number of important issues concerning cognitive development in middle childhood. In this chapter the authors:

❑ Look at the cognitive development of school-age children from the Piagetian, information-processing, and psychometric perspectives

❑ Describe advances in moral reasoning, memory, and language abilities

❑ Discuss controversies surrounding the design and use of IQ tests, bilingual education, and teaching of reading

❑ Examine influences on school achievement and how schools meet special needs

## GUIDEPOSTS FOR STUDY

13.1  How do school-age children's thinking and moral reasoning differ from those of younger children?

13.2  What advances in memory and other information-processing skills occur during middle childhood?

13.3  How accurately can schoolchildren's intelligence be measured?

13.4  How do communicative abilities and literacy expand during middle childhood?

13.5  What influences school achievement?

13.6  How do schools meet the needs of non-English-speaking children and those with learning problems?

13.7  How is giftedness assessed and nurtured?

## CHAPTER 13 REVIEW

**Section I Piagetian Approach: The Concrete Operational Child**

FRAMEWORK FOR SECTION I

A.      Cognitive Advances
   1.  Space
   2.  Causality
   3.  Categorization
   4.  Conservation
   5.  Number an Mathematics

B.      Influences of Neurological Development and Culture

C.      Moral Reasoning

## IMPORTANT TERMS FOR SECTION I

**Completion:** Fill in the blanks to complete the definitions of key terms for this section of Chapter 13.

1.  **concrete operations:** Third stage of Piagetian cognitive development (approximately from ages 7 to 12), during which children develop logical but not _____ thinking.

2.  **class _____:** Understanding of the relationship between the whole and its parts.

3. _____: Type of logical reasoning that moves from a general premise about a class to a conclusion about a particular member or members of the class.
4. _____: Type of logical reasoning that moves from particular observations to a general conclusion.
5. **seriation:** Ability to order items along a _____.
6. _____ **inference:** Understanding of the relationship between two objects by knowing the relationship of each to a third object.
7. **conservation:** In Piaget's terminology, awareness that two objects that are equal according to a certain measure (such as length, weight, or quantity) remain equal in the face of perceptual _____ (for example, a change in shape), so long as nothing has been added to or taken away from either object.
8. **horizontal décalage:** In Piaget's terminology, a child's inability to transfer learning about one type of _____ to other types, hence, the child masters different types of _____ tasks at different ages.
9. **morality of** _____: First of Piaget's two stages of moral development, characterized by rigid, simplistic judgments.
10. **morality of** _____: Second of Piaget's two stages of moral development, characterized by flexible, subtle judgments and formulation of one's own moral code.

## LEARNING OBJECTIVES FOR SECTION I

After reading and reviewing this section of Chapter 13, you should be able to do the following.

1. List and give examples of improved capabilities children achieve during the stage of concrete operations, and name one important limitation of concrete operational thought.

2. Give reasons for, and evidence of, the improvement in school-age children's spatial thinking.

3. Explain how the concept of conservation is tested, and name three principles that enter into the understanding of conservation.

4. Outline the sequence in which different types of conservation typically develop, and give three explanations for horizontal décalage.

5. Trace the development of numerical skills in middle childhood.

6. Give evidence regarding influences of culture and schooling on cognitive advances.

7. Explain the link between moral and cognitive development, and describe Piaget's two stages of moral reasoning.

## Section II Information-Processing Approach: Memory and Other Processing Skills
### FRAMEWORK FOR SECTION II

A.      Basic Processes and Capacities

B.      Metamemory: Understanding Memory

C.      Mnemonics: Strategies for Remembering

D.      Selective Attention

E.      Information Processing and Piagetian Tasks

### IMPORTANT TERMS FOR SECTION II

**Completion:** Fill in the blanks to complete the definitions of key terms for this section of Chapter 13.

1.  **working memory:** _____ -term storage of information being actively processed.
2.  **central** _____: In Baddeley's model, element of working memory that controls the processing of information.
3.  **long-term memory:** Storage of virtually _____ capacity, which holds information for very long periods.
4.  _____: Understanding of processes of memory.
5.  **mnemonic strategies:** Techniques to aid _____.
6.  _____ **memory aids:** Mnemonic strategies using something outside the person, such as a list.
7.  **rehearsal:** Mnemonic strategy to keep an item in working memory through conscious
    _____.
8.  _____: Mnemonic strategy consisting of categorizing material to be remembered.
9.  **elaboration:** Mnemonic strategy of making mental associations involving items to be remembered, sometimes with an imagined scene or _____.

## LEARNING OBJECTIVES FOR SECTION II

After reading and reviewing this section of Chapter 13, you should be able to do the following.

1. Name and describe three steps in the operation of memory (according to information-processing theory) and tell how brain's memory capacity and functioning change during middle childhood.

2. Trace progress in children's understanding of their own memory processes.

3. Identify four common mnemonic strategies and assess their effectiveness, singly or in combination.

4. Describe changes in attentional abilities in middle childhood.

5. Give examples of how improvements in information processing may help explain advances in Piagetian tasks.

6. Outline Case's theory, and explain how it draws from and differs from Piaget's.

**Section III Psychometric Approach: Assessment of Intelligence**

## FRAMEWORK FOR SECTION III

A.    Traditional Group and Individual Tests

B.    The IQ Controversy

    1.    Influence of Schooling

    2.    Influence of Ethnicity

    3.    Cultural Bias

C.    Is There More Than One Intelligence?

    1.    Gardner's Theory of Multiple Intelligences

    2.    Sternberg's Triarchic Theory of Intelligence

D.    Alternative Directions in Intelligence Testing

## IMPORTANT TERMS FOR SECTION III

**Completion:** Fill in the blanks to complete the definitions of key terms for this section of Chapter 13.

1.  _____ **tests:** Tests that measure children's general intelligence, or capacity to learn.

2.  _____ **tests:** Tests that assess how much children know in various subject areas.

3.  _____-_____ **School Ability Test:** Group intelligence test for kindergarten through twelfth grade.

4.  **Wechsler Intelligence Scale for Children (WISC-III):** Individual intelligence test for schoolchildren, which yields _____ and _____ scores as well as a combined score.

5.  _____ **Assessment Battery for Children (abbreviated \_\_\_\_\_):** Nontraditional individual intelligence test for children ages 2½ to 12½, which seeks to provide fair assessments of minority children and children with disabilities.

6.  **theory of multiple intelligences:** _____ 's theory that distinct, multiple forms of intelligence exist in each person.

7.  **triarchic theory of intelligence:** Sternberg's theory describing three types of intelligence: _____ (analytical ability), _____ (insight and originality), and _____ (practical thinking).

8.  _____ **element:** In Sternberg's triarchic theory, term for the analytic aspect of intelligence, which determines how efficiently people process information and solve problems.

9.  _____ **element:** In Sternberg's triarchic theory, term for the insightful aspect of intelligence, which determines how effectively people approach both novel and familiar tasks.

10. _____ **element:** In Sternberg's triarchic theory, term for the practical aspect of intelligence, which determines how effectively people deal with their environment.

11. **Sternberg Triarchic Abilities Test (STAT):** Test that seeks to measure _____, _____, and _____ intelligence in verbal, quantitative, and figural (spatial) domains.

12. **cultural** _____ : Tendency of intelligence tests to include items calling for knowledge or skills more familiar or meaningful to some cultural groups than to others, thus placing some test-takers at an advantage or disadvantage due to their cultural background.

13. **culture-free:** Describing an intelligence test that, if it were possible to design, would have _____ culturally linked content. Compare <u>culture-fair.</u>

14. **culture-fair:** Describing an intelligence test that deals with experiences common to various cultures, in an attempt to avoid cultural _____ . Compare <u>culture-free.</u>

## LEARNING OBJECTIVES FOR SECTION III

After reading and reviewing this section of Chapter 13, you should be able to do the following.

1. Distinguish between aptitude and achievement tests, and name and describe three commonly used intelligence tests for school-age children.


2. Discuss the pros and cons of intelligence testing.


3. Compare Gardner's theory of multiple intelligences and Sternberg's triarchic theory of intelligence; tell how they challenge the value of conventional intelligence tests; and describe a test based on Sternberg's theory.


4. Discuss factors affecting differences in IQ between white and African American children.


5. Discuss the problem of cultural bias in designing intelligence tests.


6. Explain the high achievement of schoolchildren of East Asian extraction.


**Section IV Language and Literacy**

FRAMEWORK FOR SECTION IV

A.      Vocabulary, Grammar, and Syntax

B.      Pragmatics: Knowledge about Communication

C.      Literacy
  1.   Reading
  2.   Writing

## IMPORTANT TERMS FOR SECTION IV

**Completion:** Fill in the blanks to complete the definitions of key terms for this section of Chapter 13.
  1. _____: Awareness of a person's own mental processes.

## LEARNING OBJECTIVES FOR SECTION IV

After reading and reviewing this section of Chapter 13, you should be able to do the following.
  1. Give examples of advances in schoolchildren's use and understanding of grammar and syntax.

  2. Give examples of how social interaction affects literacy.

### Section V The Child in School

## FRAMEWORK FOR SECTION V

A.      Entering First Grade
B.      Environmental Influences on School Achievement
  1.   The Family
  2.   Teacher Expectation
  3.   The Educational System
  4.   The Culture
C.      Second Language Education
D.      Children with Learning Problems
  1.   Mental Retardation
  2.   Learning disabilities
  3.   Hyperactivity and Attention Deficits
  4.   Educating Children with Disabilities
E.      Gifted Children
  1.   Identifying Gifted Children
  2.   The Lives of Gifted Children
  3.   Defining and Measuring Creativity

4. Educating Gifted, Creative, and Talented Children

## IMPORTANT TERMS FOR SECTION V

**Completion:** Fill in the blanks to complete the definitions of key terms for this section of Chapter 13.

1. **English-_____**: Approach to teaching as a second language in which instruction is presented only in English from the outset of formal education.
2. _____ **education:** A system of teaching foreign-speaking children in two languages-- their native language and English--and later switching to all-English instruction after the children develop enough fluency in English.
3. _____: Fluent in two languages.
4. **mental** _____: Significantly subnormal cognitive functioning.
5. **attention-deficit/hyperactivity disorder (ADHD):** Syndrome characterized by persistent inattention, impulsivity, low _____ for frustration, distractibility, and considerable activity at inappropriate times and places.
6. **dyslexia:** Developmental disorder in learning to _____.
7. _____ _____ **(abbreviated** _____**):** Disorders that interfere with specific aspects of learning and school achievement.
8. _____: Ability to see things in a new light, resulting in a novel product, the identification of a previously unrecognized problem, or the formulation of new and unusual solutions.
9. **convergent thinking:** Thinking aimed at finding the one "_____" answer to a problem. Compare divergent thinking.
10. _____ **thinking:** Thinking that produces a variety of fresh, diverse possibilities. Compare convergent thinking.
11. _____: Approach to educating the gifted, which broadens and deepens knowledge and skills through extra activities, projects, field trips, or mentoring.
12. _____: Approach to educating the gifted, which moves them through the entire curriculum, or part of it, at an unusually rapid pace.

## LEARNING OBJECTIVES FOR SECTION V

After reading and reviewing this section of Chapter 13, you should be able to do the following.

1. Identify characteristics of children who do well in school.

2. Compare the effectiveness of external and internal motivation, and assess the impact of parenting styles.

3. Discuss how culturally derived parental beliefs can affect children's achievement in school.

4. Discuss the relationship between socioeconomic status and school achievement.

5. Summarize recent trends in U. S. education.

6. List at least five ways to teach children thinking skills.

7. Discuss the issues involved in the controversies over second-language education and methods of teaching reading.

8. Identify three principles of the Kamehameha Early Education Program (KEEP) for children from minority cultures.

9. Discuss the incidence, causes, effects, prognosis, and treatment of mental retardation, attention-deficit/hyperactivity disorder (ADHD), and learning disabilities such as dyslexia, and state the central principle embodied in the Individuals with Disabilities Education Act.

10. Compare four ways of defining <u>giftedness.</u>

11. Summarize findings about the life success and social adjustment of gifted children.

12. Explain how creativity differs from academic intelligence, and why it is difficult to identify.

13. Identify three factors important in the development of talent.

14. Compare two approaches to educating able learners.

15. Discuss the problem of underrepresentation of minorities in programs for the gifted, and identify a fundamental dilemma regarding special education for the gifted.

# CHAPTER 13 QUIZ

**Matching--Who's Who:** Match each name in the left-hand column with the appropriate description at the right. Here, a description may be used for more than one name.

1. Jean Piaget _____
2. Whoopi Goldberg _____
3. Howard Gardner _____
4. Lev Vygotsky _____
5. Robert Sternberg _____
6. Carol S. Chomsky _____
7. Robbie Case _____
8. Thomas Edison _____
9. Nelson Rockefeller _____
10. Lewis Terman _____

a. held that intelligence results from ongoing interaction between person and environment
b. tested children's understanding of syntax
c. is believed to have had dyslexia
d. proposed two stages of moral development
e. proposed triarchic theory of intelligence
f. proposed the existence of at least seven separate "intelligences"
g. initiated a longitudinal study of gifted children
h. proposed a neo-Piagetian theory of cognitive development

**Multiple-Choice:** Circle the choice that best completes or answers each item.

1. A child in Piaget's stage of concrete operations can do <u>all but which</u> of the following?
   a. understand logical relationships
   b. classify objects
   c. distinguish between reality and fantasy
   d. think abstractly
2. "All birds have wings. A robin is a bird, therefore a robin has wings." This is an example of
   a. transitive inference
   b. deduction
   c. induction
   d. class inclusion
3. "Jeremy is taller than Julia, and Julia is taller than me, so Jeremy is taller than me." This is an example of
   a. seriation
   b. transitive inference
   c. class inclusion
   d. horizontal décalage
4. Which of the following types of conservation is generally the last to develop?
   a. volume
   b. weight
   c. substance
   d. none of the above; all of these types of conservation develop at about the same time

5. Rita has just developed a new skill. First she counts the fingers on her left hand ("1-2-3-4-5"). When asked how many fingers she has on both hands, she begins counting the fingers on her right hand, going on with "6-7-8-9-10." Rita is probably about how old?
   a. 4 or 5
   b. 6 or 7
   c. 8 or 9
   d. 10 or 11
6. According to Piaget, the factor that most strongly affects the development of conservation is
   a. intelligence
   b. maturation
   c. schooling
   d. cultural background
7. In Piaget's theory of moral reasoning, children reach the stage of morality of cooperation when they
   a. think less egocentrically
   b. accept parental standards and rules
   c. judge an act by its consequences
   d. favor severe punishment
8. Failure to remember can occur because of deficiencies in
   a. encoding
   b. storage
   c. retrieval
   d. any of the above

9. According to a widely accepted model, the central executive
    a. separates verbal and visual processing of information
    b. is part of long-term memory
    c. is located in the brain's temporal lobe
    d. is responsible for metamemory

10. Which of the following statements about metamemory is true?
    a. Until age 6, children have virtually no awareness of how their memory works.
    b. Metamemory improves steadily from kindergarten through fifth grade.
    c. Metamemory improves only slightly before third grade, then takes a big jump between third and fifth grades.
    d. Metamemory does not begin to develop until age 10 or 11.

11. Which of the following is an external aid to memory?
    a. organization
    b. elaboration
    c. writing
    d. rehearsal

12. The growth of selective attention in middle childhood is believed to be due to
    a. neurological maturation
    b. schooling
    c. improved recall
    d. more focused interests

13. Neo-Piagetian psychologists combine elements of Piaget's theory with findings of which kind of research?
    a. Vygotskian
    b. psychometric
    c. information-processing
    d. cognitive neuroscience

14. The most widely used individual intelligence test for schoolchildren is the
    a. Wechsler Intelligence Scale for Children
    b. Stanford-Binet Intelligence Scale
    c. Otis-Lennon School Ability Test
    d. Kaufman Assessment Battery for Children

15. Which of the following statements about IQ tests is true?
    a. Despite standardization, the tests have little validity or reliability.
    b. Scores are poor predictors of achievement in school.
    c. Scores are more closely related to age than to amount of schooling.
    d. Because tests are timed, children who work slowly tend to do poorly.

16. Which of Gardner's "intelligences" is best measured by traditional intelligence tests?
    a. musical
    b. spatial
    c. bodily-kinesthetic
    d. linguistic

17. According to Sternberg's triarchic theory, which element of intelligence is required for most tasks in school?
    a. componential
    b. experiential
    c. contextual
    d. figural

18. Test developers have been unable to devise culture-fair intelligence tests because
    a. tests require the use of language
    b. it is impossible to eliminate culture-linked content
    c. "common" experiences are affected by cultural values
    d. all of the above

19. Which of the following sentence constructions would a 6-year-old be most likely to use?
    a. "I knew that the teacher was going to call on me."
    b. "These cookies were baked yesterday."
    c. "If my father was here, he'd beat you up."
    d. "I have looked all over for my ball, and I can't find it."

20. According to one study, which fourth-grader is likely to write a story with fewer errors and more elaborate ideas and to concentrate better on the task?
    a. a boy working alone
    b. a girl working alone
    c. a child working with friend
    d. a child working with classmate who is not a friend

21. Elena, whose native language is Spanish, is learning academic subjects in Spanish until her English becomes more fluent. Elena is being taught according to which of the following approaches?
    a. English-immersion
    b. bilingual education
    c. dual language
    d. code switching

22. Which of the following is likely to do best in the early grades of school?
    a. Anne, who always does what the teacher tells her to do
    b. Barry, who fidgets in his seat
    c. Carol, who frequently speaks up in class
    d. Doug, who is extremely polite

23. Which of the following parents is most likely to have a child who is a high achiever?
    a. Alice, who expects her daughter to do well in school and gives her extra allowance when she does
    b. Brenda, who puts pressure on her son to do well but doesn't really expect him to
    c. Curt, who expects his daughter to do well and punishes her when she falls short
    d. David, who encourages his son's interest in the work

24. Experience with the Kamehameha Early Education Program (KEEP) suggests that teachers can help children from minority cultures feel more comfortable and achieve more by doing all but which of the following?
    a. teaching subject matter important in the students' cultures
    b. matching their own patterns and rhythms of speech to the students'
    c. letting students teach and learn from each other
    d. adjusting for culturally influenced learning styles

25. About how many children in the United States are identified as learning disabled?
    a. 20,000 to 30,000
    b. 100,000 to 200 thousand
    c. 1 million
    d. more than 2 million

26. The Individuals with Disabilities Education Act requires placement of children with disabilities, whenever possible, in
    a. residential programs
    b. special schools
    c. special classes
    d. the least restrictive environment

27. Identification of giftedness may be based on
    a. an IQ score of 130 or higher
    b. outstanding ability in a specific area such as math or science
    c. creative thinking
    d. any of the above

28. Gifted children tend to have social and emotional problems if their IQs are higher than
    a. 130
    b. 150
    c. 180
    d. 200

29. Tests of creativity attempt to measure
    a. convergent thinking
    b. divergent thinking
    c. subjective thinking
    d. artistic talent

**True or False?** In the blank following each item, write T (for true) or F (for false). In the space below each item, if the statement is false, rewrite it to make it true.

1. According to Piaget, the ability to think abstractly develops in the stage of concrete operations, which coincides with middle childhood. _____

2. A team captain who lines up team members in order of height is showing sequential processing. _____

3. Research has established that children in nonwestern cultures tend to achieve conservation later than children in western cultures because their cultures place less importance on this ability. _____

4. In Piaget's stage of morality of constraint, children believe that an act is bad if it is punished. _____

5. When second-graders try to remember a list of items, they are more likely to categorize the information than to repeat it over and over. _____

6. Selective attention helps children avoid mistakes in recall. _____

7. One criticism of IQ tests is that they fail to separate aptitude from achievement. _____

8. African Americans, on average, score 15 points lower on IQ tests than white Americans. _____

9. The explanation for the high achievement of Asian schoolchildren is that they start out with a cognitive advantage. _____

10. Children's understanding of syntax continues to develop until the age of 9 or later. _____

11. Kindergartners sometimes are unaware that when they do not understand directions they cannot do a job well. _____

12. Children's attitudes toward reading become less positive after first grade. _____

13. Research has established the superiority of the whole-language method of teaching reading. _____

14. The "back to basics" trend in education was inspired by a drop in high school students' SAT scores during the mid-1970s. _____

15. The ability to think is inborn and cannot be taught. _____

16. Mental retardation and hyperactivity are more commonly diagnosed in boys than in girls. _____

17. Children with learning disabilities tend to have below-average intelligence. _____

18. With proper guidance, a child can outgrow a learning disability. _____

19. Creativity and IQ are highly correlated. _____

20. There is little or no evidence that tests of creativity, such as the Torrance Tests of Creative Thinking, are reliable. _____

# ANSWER KEY FOR CHAPTER 13

## CHAPTER 13 REVIEW

### Important Terms for Section I
1. abstract
2. inclusion
3. deductive
4. inductive
5. dimension
6. transitive
7. alteration
8. conservation, conservation
9. constraint
10. cooperation

### Important Terms for Section II
1. short
2. executive
3. unlimited
4. metamemory
5. memory
6. external
7. repetition
8. organization
9. story

### Important Terms for Section III
1. aptitude
2. achievement
3. Otis-Lennon
4. verbal, performance
5. Kaufman, K-ABC
6. Gardner
7. componential, experiential, contextual
8. componential
9. experiential
10. contextual
11. componential, experiential, contextual
12. bias
13. no
14. bias

### Important Terms for Section IV
1. metacognition

### Important Terms for Section V
1. immersion
2. bilingual
3. bilingual
4. retardation

5. tolerance
6. read
7. learning disabilities (LDs)
8. creativity
9. right
10. divergent
11. enrichment
12. acceleration

## CHAPTER 13 QUIZ

### Matching--Who's Who
1. d
2. c
3. f
4. a
5. e
6. b
7. h
8. c
9. c
10. g

### Multiple-Choice
1. d
2. b
3. b
4. a
5. b
6. b
7. a
8. d
9. a
10. b
11. c
12. a
13. c
14. a
15. d
16. d
17. a
18. c
19. a
20. c
21. b
22. c
23. d
24. a
25. d

26. d
27. d
28. c
29. b

## True or False?

1. F-According to Piaget, the ability to think abstractly does not develop until adolescence.
2. F-The captain is showing an understanding of seriation.
3. F-More recent research suggests that when nonwestern children are tested by examiners from their own culture, who speak their language, they do about as well on conservation tasks as a comparison group.
4. T
5. F-Second-graders tend to use rehearsal spontaneously, but children ordinarily do not use organization spontaneously until age 10 or 11.
6. T
7. T
8. T
9. F-Asian children show no early cognitive superiority; their superior performance seems to be related to educational and cultural differences.
10. T
11. T
12. T
13. F-Research has found little support for the claims of the whole-language approach.
14. T
15. F-Research shows that children can be taught to think more effectively.
16. T
17. F-Children with learning disabilities often have near-average or above average intelligence but have trouble processing sensory information.
18. F-Learning disabilities are not outgrown, but people can learn to cope with them.
19. F-Studies have found only modest correlations between creativity and IQ.
20. F-The Torrance Tests are fairly reliable, but there is little evidence that they are valid.

# CHAPTER 14
# PSYCHOSOCIAL DEVELOPMENT IN MIDDLE CHILDHOOD

## OVERVIEW

Chapter 14 describes the rich, expanding social world of middle childhood and the personality changes children experience during these years. In this chapter, the authors:

❑ Discuss how self-concept, self-esteem, and emotional control develop during middle childhood

❑ Describe changes in parent-child relationships during these years

❑ Assess the impact on children of parents' employment, of divorce and remarriage, of gay and lesbian parents, of poverty, and of other contextual factors

❑ Discuss how siblings affect each other's development

❑ Describe the formation, composition, and influence of peer groups

❑ Examine the bases of popularity and friendship

❑ Describe common emotional disturbances and their treatment

❑ Identify factors contributing to stress and resilience

## GUIDEPOSTS FOR STUDY

14.1  How do school-age children develop a realistic self-concept and what contributes to self-esteem?

14.2  How do school-age children show emotional growth?

14.3  How do parent-child relationships change in middle childhood?

14.4  What are the effects of parents' work and of poverty on family atmosphere?

14.5  What impact does family structure have on children's development?

14.6  How do siblings influence and get along with each other?

14.7  How do relationships with peers change in middle childhood and what influences popularity and choice of friends?

14.8  What are the most common forms of aggressive behavior in middle childhood and what influences contribute to them?

14.9  What are some common emotional disturbances and how are they treated?

14.10  How do the stresses of modern life affect children and what enables "resilient" children to withstand them?

## CHAPTER 14 REVIEW

### Section I The Developing Self

FRAMEWORK FOR SECTION I

A.  Representational Systems: A Neo-Piagetian View

B.  Self-Esteem

C.  Emotional Growth

## IMPORTANT TERMS FOR SECTION I

**Completion:** Fill in the blanks to complete the definitions of key terms for this section of Chapter 14.

1. **representational** _____: In neo-Piagetian terminology, the third stage in development of self-definition, characterized by breadth, balance, and the integration and assessment of various aspects of the self.

2. **industry versus inferiority:** In Erikson's theory, the fourth critical alternative of psychosocial development, occurring during middle childhood, in which children must learn the productive _____ their culture requires or else face feelings of inferiority.

## LEARNING OBJECTIVES FOR SECTION I

After reading and reviewing this section of Chapter 14, you should be able to do the following.

1. Explain the significance of the development of representational systems during middle childhood.

2. Describe personality characteristics of children with high and low self-esteem, and discuss Erikson's views and Harter's findings on its sources.

3. Tell how parenting styles influence self-esteem.

4. Discuss aspects of emotional growth in middle childhood, including the understanding and control of negative emotions and the increase in empathy and prosocial behavior.

## Section II The Child in the Family

## FRAMEWORK FOR SECTION II

A.      Family Atmosphere
    1.   Parenting Issues: Coregulation and Discipline

2. Effects of Parents' Work

3. Poverty and Parenting

B. Family Structure
   1. Traditional and Nontraditional Families: An Overview
   2. Adoptive Families
   3. When Parents Divorce
   4. Living in a One-Parent Family
   5. Living in a Stepfamily
   6. Living with Gay and Lesbian Parents
   7. Sibling Relationships

## IMPORTANT TERM FOR SECTION II

**Completion:** Fill in the blank to complete the definition of the key term for this section of Chapter 14.

1. **coregulation:** _____ stage in the control of behavior in which parents exercise general supervision and children exercise moment-to-moment self-regulation.

## LEARNING OBJECTIVES FOR SECTION II

After reading and reviewing this section of Chapter 14, you should be able to do the following.

1. Summarize the roles of family atmosphere and family structure in children's behavior and adjustment.

2. Compare the importance to school-age children of relationships with parents, peers, and extended family, and discuss how cultural patterns influence the importance of these relationships.

3. Describe how control of behavior in middle childhood gradually shifts from parent to child, and how coregulation affects methods of discipline.

4. Identify factors influencing the effects of parents' employment on children.

195

5. Analyze effects of poverty on parenting and on children's well-being.

6. Explain why an intact family is usually the most beneficial setting for a child.

7. Discuss how divorce affects children; list six "tasks" of adjustment; identify factors that influence children's adjustment; and summarize research on long-term effects of divorce.

8. Give statistics on the prevalence of single-parent families, identify three causes for the formation of such families, and discuss apparent effects of being raised in such a family.

9. Describe special characteristics of stepfamilies, and identify factors affecting children's adjustment to life in a stepfamily.

10. Summarize research on the psychosocial development of children raised by gay and lesbian parents.

11. Give examples of how school-age siblings influence each other, both directly and indirectly.

12. Compare the roles and relationships of siblings in industrialized and nonindustrialized societies.

## Section III The Child in the Peer Group
## FRAMEWORK FOR SECTION III
A.   Positive and Negative Effects of Peer Relations
B.   Popularity
C.   Friendship
D.   Aggression and Bullying
    1.   Aggression and Social Information Processing
    2.   Does Televised Violence Lead to Aggression?
    3.   Bullies and Victims

## IMPORTANT TERMS FOR SECTION III

**Completion:** Fill in the blank to complete the definitions of key terms for this section of Chapter 14.

1. _____: Unfavorable attitude toward members of certain groups outside one's own, especially racial or ethnic groups.

2. _____ **aggression:** Aggression aimed at damaging or interfering with another person's relationships, reputation, or psychological well-being; also called covert, indirect, or psychological aggression.

3. _____: Aggression deliberately and persistently directed against a particular target, or victim, who is weak, vulnerable, and defenseless.

## LEARNING OBJECTIVES FOR SECTION III

After reading and reviewing this section of Chapter 14, you should be able to do the following.

1. Explain how peer groups form, and identify positive and negative influences of peer groups.

2. Describe characteristics of popular and unpopular children, and discuss personal, family, and cultural influences on popularity.

3. Discuss the benefits of friendship and its characteristics in middle childhood.

4. List and give examples of Selman's five stages of friendship.

5. Explain the relationship between aggression and social information processing, and explain what is meant by a hostile bias.

6. Distinguish between overt and relational aggression, and tell which is more typical among boys and which among girls.

7. Explain how patterns of bullying and choice of victims become established, identify typical characteristics of bullies and victims, and describe developmental changes in bullying and victimization.

**Section IV Mental Health**

## FRAMEWORK FOR SECTION IV

A.  Common Emotional Disturbances
   1. Disruptive Behavior Disorders
   2. School Phobia and Other Anxiety Disorders
   3. Childhood Depression

B.  Treatment Techniques
C.  Stress and Resilience
   1. Stresses of Modern Life
   2. Coping with Stress: The Resilient Child

## IMPORTANT TERMS FOR SECTION IV

**Completion:** Fill in the blanks to complete the definitions of key terms for this section of Chapter 14.

1. **school _____:** Unrealistic fear of going to school; may be a form of separation anxiety disorder.
2. **separation anxiety disorder:** Condition involving excessive, prolonged anxiety concerning separation from home or from people to whom a child is _____.
3. **childhood depression:** Affective disorder characterized by such symptoms as a prolonged sense of friendlessness, inability to have fun or concentrate, fatigue, extreme activity or apathy, feelings of worthlessness, weight change, physical complaints, and thoughts of death or _____.
4. **individual psychotherapy:** Psychological treatment in which a therapist sees a troubled person one-on-one, to help the patient gain _____ into his or her personality, relationships, feelings, and behavior.
5. **family therapy:** Psychological treatment in which a therapist sees the whole family _____ to analyze patterns of family functioning.
6. **behavior therapy:** Therapeutic approach using principles of learning theory to encourage desired behaviors or eliminate undesired ones; also called <u>behavior</u> _____.
7. **drug therapy:** Administration of drugs to treat _____ _____.
8. **_____ children:** Children who weather adverse circumstances, function well despite challenges or threats, or bounce back from traumatic events that would have a highly negative impact on the emotional development of most children.

## LEARNING OBJECTIVES FOR SECTION IV

After reading and reviewing this section of Chapter 14, you should be able to do the following.

1. Describe symptoms and treatment of school phobia.

2. List at least five symptoms of childhood depression.

3. Discuss the effectiveness of individual psychotherapy, family therapy, behavior therapy, and drug therapy.

4. Identify at least three major sources of childhood stress in modern life.

5. Name the most common childhood fear.

6. Identify five factors that seem to contribute to resilience in children.

# CHAPTER 14 QUIZ

**Matching**--Aspects of Psychosocial Development: Match each situation in the left-hand column with the most appropriate term in the right-hand column.

1. At the beginning of the school year, Mark's teacher asks the children in the class to tell something about themselves. When it is Mark's turn, he says, "I'm pretty good at sports, but I have trouble with spelling." _____

2. Caren and a friend are playing in Caren's room. Toys and books are piled everywhere. The girls want to play a game, but Caren cannot find it. "I'm not as orderly as I'd like to be," she says apologetically. _____

3. Gordon is making New Year's resolutions for a school assignment. "Stop teasing my sister," he writes at the top of the list. _____

4. Jim is alone in the candy section of a supermarket. "No one's looking," he thinks, as he takes a piece of bubble gum and puts it in his pocket. "No, that's not right," he tells himself as he changes his mind and puts it back. _____

5. Dana is playing tennis. Trying to put away an overhead shot, she hits the ball into the net. "That's OK," she tells herself, "I can make the next one." _____

6. Tim and his buddies are hanging around a music store, which is having a sidewalk sale. While the clerk is distracted, some of the boys take cassettes out of a bin and put them in their pockets. Tim, seeing his friends do this, grabs a cassette even though he knows he shouldn't.

   _____

7. Jeremy comes home from school and finds a note from his mother: "Please remember to water the plants and clean up your room." Jeremy is tired and would rather watch television right away, but because of his mother's reminder, he does his chores first.

   _____

a. self-esteem

b. coregulation

c. representational systems

d. self-regulation

e. conformity

f. prosocial behavior

g. comparing real self with ideal self

**Multiple-Choice:** Circle the choice that best completes or answers each item.

1. <u>All but which</u> of the following may be part of the self-concept?
   a. "I am a good athlete."
   b. "I am a hard worker."
   c. "I have trouble making friends."
   d. "I don't like Tracy."

2. The "virtue" that arises from successful resolution of Erikson's crisis of industry versus inferiority is
   a. productivity
   b. self-confidence
   c. competence
   d. industriousness

3. According to Harter's research, the greatest contributor to self-esteem in 8- to 12-year-olds is
   a. regard by parents and classmates
   b. competence in schoolwork
   c. athletic skills
   d. good conduct

4. Parents of children with high self-esteem tend to use which parenting style?
   a. authoritarian
   b. permissive
   c. authoritative
   d. any of the above; no relationship has been found between parenting style and self-esteem

5. <u>All but which</u> of the following statements about emotional growth in middle childhood are true?
   a. Internalization of shame and pride have occurred.
   b. Children are more empathic than before.
   c. Children have more control of their emotions than before.
   d. Children are more wary of showing negative feelings to parents than to friends.

6. Which of the following factors most strongly affects children's adjustment?
   a. marital status of the parents
   b. number of parents in the home
   c. mother's employment
   d. atmosphere in the home

7. Parents of school-age children are most likely to use which of the following kinds of discipline?
   a. inductive
   b. deductive
   c. power assertion
   d. withdrawal of love

8. About what proportion of married women with school-age children are in the work force?
   a. 30 percent
   b. 50 percent
   c. 75 percent
   d. 90 percent

9. About how many school-age "self-care children" of working parents are there in the United States?
   a. fewer than 1 million
   b. 2 million
   c. 10 million
   d. 20 million

10. Husbands of working mothers tend to be most involved with the child(ren) when
    a. there is only one child
    b. the mother works part-time
    c. the children are school-age
    d. the mother earns close to what the father does

11. In comparison with children of a full-time homemaker, school-age children of a working mother generally
    a. have lower self-esteem
    b. live in less structured homes
    c. are more independent
    d. resent their mother's absence

12. Which of the following proposed an ecological analysis of effects of poverty?
    a. Urie Bronfenbrenner
    b. Susan Harter
    c. Vonnie McLoyd
    d. Robert Selman

13. What proportion of children under 18 in the United States live with both biological or adoptive parents?
    a. less than 25 percent
    b. about 50 percent
    c. more than 60 percent
    d. 75 percent

14. <u>All but which</u> of the following are emotional "tasks" that face children of divorce?
    a. acknowledging the reality of the divorce
    b. resuming customary pursuits
    c. resolving anger and self-blame
    d. being wary of intimate relationships

15. Which of the following statements about children's adjustment to divorce is true, according to research?
    a. Children of authoritarian parents usually have fewer behavior problems than those with authoritative or permissive parents.
    b. The best custody arrangement is joint custody.
    c. Boys tend to have more adjustment problems than girls when their mothers remarry.
    d. As adults, children of divorced parents tend to have lower socioeconomic status than adults who grew up in intact families.

16. Which country has the lowest percentage of single-parent families?
    a. Australia
    b. France
    c. Japan
    d. Sweden

17. Which is the major source of single-parent families in the United States today?
    a. divorce
    b. death of the mother
    c. death of the father
    d. unwed motherhood

18. According to one large-scale study, which of the following factors has a more negative effect on school achievement?
    a. single-parent home
    b. low income
    c. both have equally negative effect
    d. neither has a strongly negative effect

19. As compared with children of heterosexual parents, children living with homosexual parents are more likely to
    a. have psychological problems
    b. be abused
    c. be homosexual themselves
    d. none of the above

20. The combination of siblings likely to quarrel most is
    a. two brothers
    b. two sisters
    c. a brother and sister
    d. none of the above; all quarrel equally

21. All but which of the following are benefits of the peer group?
    a. realistic gauge of abilities
    b. sense of identity
    c. opportunity to test values
    d. development of coregulation

22. In middle childhood, popular children tend to have all but which of the following?
    a. strong cognitive abilities
    b. superior social skills
    c. strong interest in the other sex
    d. assertiveness

23. Which of the following children is likely to be unpopular?
    a. Audrey, who is disciplined by punishment and threats
    b. Bonita, who is disciplined by reasoning
    c. Claudia, who is disciplined by withdrawal of love
    d. Danielle, who is rarely disciplined

24. At which of Selman's levels of friendship would a child say, "He wouldn't let me watch television at his house, so he's not my friend anymore"?
    a. undifferentiated
    b. unilateral
    c. reciprocal
    d. mutual

25. Janice brought her new flute to school, and the teacher let her play for the class. "What a show-off," Sarah whispered to the girls around her. "Let's not play with her at recess." This is an example of
    a. hostile aggression
    b. instrumental aggression
    c. overt aggression
    d. relational aggression

26. Mental health problems of U.S. 7- to 16-year-olds have increased in all but which of the following areas?
    a. withdrawal or social problems
    b. aggression or delinquency
    c. anxiety or depression
    d. fears, guilt, and bodily complaints

27. School-phobic children tend to be
    a. boys
    b. low achievers
    c. willful, stubborn, and demanding at home
    d. difficult to treat

28. Behavior therapy is based on which theoretical perspective?
    a. psychoanalytic
    b. learning
    c. contextual
    d. cognitive
29. David Elkind has studied characteristics of which kind of child?
    a. resilient
    b. "hurried"
    c. maltreated
    d. school-phobic
30. According to surveys, fears of school-age children most often center on
    a. health
    b. school
    c. personal harm
    d. psychological stress

**True or False?** In the blank following each item, write T (for true) or F (for false). In the space below each item, if the statement is false, rewrite it to make it true.

1. School-age children have trouble recognizing apparently contradictory aspects of themselves. _____

2. When 8- to 12-year-old children evaluate themselves, they give the most importance to physical appearance. _____

3. According to some research, school-age children spend only about half an hour a day interacting with their parents. _____

4. As children become preadolescents, the quality of family problem solving improves. _____

5. Parents' approach to child rearing generally changes as children grow older. _____

6. Children tend to be adversely affected by their mothers' employment. _____

7. Self-care children generally live with poor single parents in urban neighborhoods. _____

8. Husbands of working mothers tend to be more involved in housework and child care than husbands of at-home mothers. _____

9. Children tend to do better in intact families. _____

10. Children often blame themselves for their parents' divorce. _____

11. The final task children face, in their adjustment to divorce, is accepting its permanence. _____

12. Children whose parents have joint custody generally adjust to divorce better than those who are in sole custody of one parent. _____

13. During the 1980s, the number of father-only families grew three times as fast as the number of mother-only families. _____

14. Boys tend to have more trouble than girls in accepting a stepfather. _____

15. Younger siblings tend to be good at sensing other people's needs. _____

16. Elder siblings more regularly take care of younger ones in nonindustrialized than in industrialized societies. _____

17. A study of school-age children in Montreal found that ethnic prejudice increases with age. _____

18. In China, sensitive, shy children tend to be unpopular during middle childhood.

_____

19. During middle childhood, friends disagree more than children who are not friends. _____

20. Children who are victims of bullies often continue to be victimized even when they have different classmates. _____

21. A child who exhibits school phobia should be allowed to stay home until the phobia subsides. _____

22. Ten-year-olds frequently make up stories about their exploits and lie to avoid punishment. _____

23. In family therapy, the child whose problem causes the family to seek treatment is sometimes the healthiest member. _____

24. Drug therapy is treatment for drug addiction. _____

25. Therapy for specific problems tends to be more effective than therapy aimed at improving social adjustment in general. _____

26. Children generally take frequent moves in stride. _____

27. School is a source of worry for many children. _____

28. Resilient children are likely to have at least one close relationship with a competent, caring adult. _____

# ANSWER KEY FOR CHAPTER 14

## CHAPTER 14 REVIEW

**Important Terms for Section I**
1. systems
2. skills

**Important Term for Section II**
1. transitional

**Important Terms for Section III**
1. prejudice
2. relational
3. bullying

**Important Terms for Section IV**
1. phobia
2. attached
3. suicide
4. insight
5. together
6. modification
7. emotional disorders
8. resilient

## CHAPTER 14 QUIZ

**Matching--Aspects of Psychosocial Development**
1. c
2. g
3. f
4. d
5. a
6. e
7. b

**Multiple-Choice**
1. d
2. c
3. a
4. c
5. d
6. d
7. a
8. c
9. b
10. d
11. c
12. c
13. c
14. d
15. d
16. c
17. d
18. b
19. d
20. a
21. d
22. c
23. a
24. b
25. d
26. d
27. c
28. b
29. b
30. c

**True or False?**
1. F-School-age children can form self-concepts that integrate contradictory aspects of the self.
2. T
3. T
4. F-As children become preadolescents, family problem solving often deteriorates.
5. F-Although issues and disciplinary methods change somewhat as children get older, parents' basic approach to child rearing generally does not.
6. F-The effect of mothers' employment depends on many factors, such as the child's age, sex, temperament, and personality; whether the mother works full or part time, and for how many hours; whether she has a supportive or unsupportive mate, or none; the family's socioeconomic status; and the kind of care the child receives.
7. F-Many self-care children are from well-educated, middle- to upper-class families in suburban or rural areas.
8. T
9. T
10. T
11. F-The final task children face in their adjustment to divorce is achieving realistic hope about their own intimate relationships.

12. F-Joint custody does not seem to help children adjust to divorce and may worsen the situation when the divorce has been bitter.
13. T
14. F-Girls tend to have more trouble than boys in accepting a stepfather.
15. T
16. T
17. F-A study of school-age children in Montreal found that ethnic prejudice decreases with age.
18. F-In China, sensitive, shy children tend to be popular before age 12.
19. T
20. T
21. F-Children with school phobia should return to school as quickly (but gradually) as possible.
22. F-Children who continue to tell tall tales or lie frequently after the age of 6 or 7 may be acting out emotional problems.
23. T
24. F-Drug therapy is the treatment of emotional disorders with drugs.
25. T
26. F-Children who have moved 3 or more times are more at risk of emotional, behavioral, school, and health problems.
27. T
28. T

# PHYSICAL DEVELOPMENT AND HEALTH IN ADOLESCENCE

## OVERVIEW

Chapter 15 sketches the enormous physical changes that occur during adolescence. In this chapter, the authors:

❑ Identify markers of adolescence, and point out opportunities and risks of this developmental transition

❑ Describe how puberty begins, and identify possible causes and effects of variations in its timing

❑ Describe characteristic physical changes in males and females and psychological impacts of these changes

❑ Examine health issues and concerns, including the importance of physical fitness and the causes, implications, prevention, and treatment of depression, eating disorders, drug abuse, sexually transmitted diseases, and abuse and neglect

❑ Identify the chief causes of death in adolescence; discuss trends and patterns in suicide among teenagers, and suggest methods of prevention

❑ Identify protective factors affecting adolescents' health and well-being.

## GUIDEPOSTS FOR STUDY

15.1 What is adolescence and when does it begin and end?

15.2 What opportunities and risks does adolescence entail?

15.3 What physical changes do adolescents experience and how do these changes affect them psychologically?

15.4 What are some common health problems and health risks of adolescence and how can they be prevented?

## CHAPTER 15 REVIEW

### Section I Adolescence: A Developmental Transition

FRAMEWORK FOR SECTION I

A.     Markers of Adolescence

B.     Opportunities and Risks of Adolescence

IMPORTANT TERMS FOR SECTION I

**Completion:** Fill in the blanks to complete the definitions of key terms for this section of Chapter 15.

1. **adolescence:** Developmental transition between childhood and _____ entailing major physical, cognitive, and psychosocial changes.

2. **puberty:** Process by which a person attains sexual maturity and the ability to _____.

LEARNING OBJECTIVES FOR SECTION I

After reading and reviewing this section of Chapter 15, you should be able to do the following.

1. Explain why it is difficult to precisely demarcate adolescence, and identify three kinds of markers for entrance into adulthood.

2. Identify opportunities for growth during adolescence and special risks during that period.

## Section II Puberty The End of Childhood

### FRAMEWORK FOR SECTION II

A.  How Puberty Begins
B.  Timing, Sequence, and Signs of Maturation
    1.  The Adolescent Growth Spurt
    2.  Primary and Secondary Sex Characteristics
    3.  Signs of Sexual Maturity: Sperm Production and Menstruation
    4.  Sexual Attraction
C.  Psychological Effects of Early and Late Maturation

### IMPORTANT TERMS FOR SECTION II

**Completion:** Fill in the blanks to complete the definitions of key terms for this section of Chapter 15.

1. _____ **trend:** Trend that can be seen by observing several generations, such as the trend toward earlier attainment of adult height and sexual maturity, which began a century ago.
2. **adolescent growth spurt:** Sharp increase in _____ and _____ that precedes sexual maturity.
3. _____**sex characteristics:** Organs directly related to reproduction, which enlarge and mature during adolescence. Compare _____ <u>sex characteristics.</u>
4. _____ **sex characteristics:** Physiological signs of sexual maturation (such as breast development and growth of body hair) that do not involve the sex organs. Compare _____ <u>sex characteristics.</u>
5. **spermarche:** Boy's first _____.
6. **menarche:** Girl's first _____.
7. **gonadarche:  Maturation of** _____ **or** _____.

### LEARNING OBJECTIVES FOR SECTION II

After reading and reviewing this section of Chapter 15, you should be able to do the following.

1. Describe the onset of puberty, tell what may bring it on, and discuss the role of hormonal changes.

2. State the duration and range of ages of onset of puberty in boys and girls.

3. Define the secular trend and identify its most likely cause.

4. Describe the major physical changes that precede or signal sexual maturity in boys and in girls, and list the sequence in which they occur.

5. Describe what happens during the adolescent growth spurt.

6. Distinguish between primary and secondary sex characteristics, and describe how they change during puberty.

7. Tell how adolescents react to spermarche and menarche.

8. Identify adolescent girls' and boys' main concerns about physical appearance.

9. Compare psychological effects of early and late maturation in boys and in girls.

## Section III Physical and Mental Health
## FRAMEWORK FOR SECTION III

A.  Physical Activity

B.  Sleep Needs

C.  Nutrition and Eating Disorders
1.  Obesity
2.  Body Image
3.  Anorexia Nervosa
4.  Bulimia Nervosa
5.  Treatments and Outcomes for Anorexia and Bulima

D.  Use and Abuse of Drugs
1.  Trends and Factors in Drug Use
2.  Gateway Drugs: Alcohol, Marijuana, and Tobacco

E.  Sexually Transmitted Diseases (STDs)

F.  Abuse and Neglect

G.  Death in Adolescence
1.  Deaths from Vehicle Accidents and Firearms
2.  Suicide

H.  Protective Factors: Health in Context

## IMPORTANT TERMS FOR SECTION III

**Completion:** Fill in the blanks to complete the definitions of key terms for this section of Chapter 15.

1. _____ **nervosa:** Eating disorder characterized by self-starvation.

2. _____ **nervosa:** Eating disorder in which a person regularly eats huge quantities of food and then purges the body by laxatives, induced vomiting, fasting, or excessive exercise.

3. **substance** _____: Repeated, harmful use of a substance, usually alcohol or another drug.

4. **substance** _____: Addiction (physical or psychological, or both) to a harmful substance.

5. **gateway drugs:** Drugs such as alcohol, tobacco, and marijuana, the use of which tends to lead to use of more _____ drugs.

6. **sexually transmitted diseases or infections (STDs):** Diseases spread by sexual contact; also called _____ diseases.

## LEARNING OBJECTIVES FOR SECTION III

After reading and reviewing this section of Chapter 15, you should be able to do the following.

1. Summarize health and fitness concerns about adolescents, particularly the influence of poverty on access to health care.

2. Point out risks of athletic activity, especially for girls, and dangers of inactivity.

3. Give reasons why adolescent girls are more at risk of depression than adolescent boys.

4. Identify common nutritional deficiencies of adolescents.

5. Describe three common eating disorders--obesity, anorexia nervosa, and bulimia nervosa--and discuss their causes, effects, and treatment.

6. Discuss trends, patterns, and consequences of drug use and abuse by adolescents, particularly with regard to alcohol, marijuana, and tobacco.

7. Identify symptoms, effects, and treatment of the most prevalent sexually transmitted diseases, discuss reasons for their high incidence among adolescents, and list suggestions for prevention.

8. Discuss the incidence and effects of abuse and neglect of adolescents.

9. Name the three leading causes of death in adolescence, and differentiate death rates and causes by sex and race.

10. Identify risk factors for suicide among adolescents, and list suggestions for prevention.

11. Identify protective factors that tend to prevent risky behaviors.

# CHAPTER 15 QUIZ

**Matching--Health Issues:** Match each term in the left-hand column with the appropriate description at the right.

1. Genital herpes simplex _____

2. Anorexia nervosa _____

3. AIDS _____

4. Alcohol _____

5. Chlamydia _____

6. Obesity _____

7. Trichomoniasis _____

8. Tobacco _____

9. Genital warts (human papilloma virus) _____

10. Bulimia nervosa _____

11. Syphilis _____

12. Marijuana _____

a. eating disorder producing tooth decay and gastric irritation

b. failure of the immune system, caused by a virus transmitted through interpersonal exchanges of bodily fluids

c. drug used by about 8 out of 10 high school seniors

d. most common eating disorder in the United States

e. drug linked with lung cancer

f. eating disorder characterized by self-starvation and distorted body image

g. most prevalent curable STD in the United States

h. small, painless growths; may be most prevalent STD

i. drug that can impede memory

j. STD that can lead to paralysis, convulsions, brain damage, and sometimes death

k. highly contagious, painful blisters with no known cure

l. Parasitic infection sometimes transmitted in moist objects, such as wet towels

**Multiple-Choice:** Circle the choice that best completes or answers each item.

1. The end of adolescence is
   a. no longer an important marker of development
   b. less clear-cut in western industrial societies than before the twentieth century
   c. legally defined as age 18 in the United States for purposes of enlistment in the armed forces
   d. mainly a physiological phenomenon

2. About what proportion of adolescents are at risk of major problems?
   a. 1 out of 10
   b. 1 out of 5
   c. 1 out of 3
   d. 1 out of 2

3. The average age at which boys enter puberty is
   a. 10
   b. 12
   c. 13
   d. 14

4. The average age of onset of puberty
   a. has been dropping in the United States, western Europe, and Japan during the past 100 years
   b. is earlier in less developed countries than in less industrialized ones
   c. is earlier among white girls than among African American girls
   d. is earlier among thin girls than among overweight girls

5. The adolescent growth spurt often results in
   a. awkwardness
   b. disproportionate body parts
   c. nearsightedness
   d. all of the above

6. Which of the following are primary sex characteristics?
   a. pubic and underarm hair
   b. ovaries
   c. breasts
   d. all of the above

7. One of the first signs of puberty in girls is usually
    a. menstruation
    b. budding of the breasts
    c. underarm hair
    d. oily skin, leading to acne
8. According to some research, early-maturing girls are more likely than later-maturing girls to
    a. have a good body image
    b. be sociable and poised
    c. react positively to menarche
    d. associate with antisocial peers
9. Who is the most likely to suffer from depression?
    a. Aaron, who was cut from the football team
    b. Belinda, who has acne and experienced menarche the day she entered high school
    c. Cory, whose girlfriend just broke up with him
    d. Any of the above
10. The average teenage girl needs about how many calories per day?
    a. 1,200
    b. 1,500
    c. 1,900
    d. 2,200
11. About what proportion of adolescents in the United States are obese?
    a. 1 in 5
    b. 1 in 10
    c. 1 in 20
    d. 1 in 50
12. The cause of anorexia nervosa is
    a. social pressure
    b. psychological disturbance
    c. physical disorder
    d. unknown
13. A sign of bulimia nervosa is
    a. loss of hair
    b. abnormal thinness
    c. eating very little
    d. each of the above
14. Overall, drug use among adolescents in the United States
    a. is more prevalent than ever before
    b. peaked during the 1960s and has declined ever since
    c. declined during the late 1980s but then increased during the 1990s
    d. increased during the late 1980s but decreased in the early 1990s

15. The most widely used illicit drug in the United States is
    a. hashish
    b. cocaine
    c. heroin
    d. marijuana
16. Which of the following statements about the virus that causes AIDS is (are) true?
    a. It is always fatal.
    b. It has no known cure.
    c. Most victims worldwide are homosexual.
    d. all of the above
17. Which sexually transmitted disease has the following early symptoms: reddish-brown sores on the mouth or genitalia, and then a widespread skin rash?
    a. syphilis
    b. herpes
    c. gonorrhea
    d. AIDS
18. Parents who maltreat adolescents tend to be
    a. authoritarian
    b. overindulgent
    c. either a or b
    d. neither a nor b
19. The leading cause of death among 15- to 24-year-olds in the United States is
    a. suicide
    b. homicide
    c. accidents
    d. drug overdoses
20. Teenagers who succeed in committing suicide are most likely to use which method?
    a. barbiturates
    b. ingesting poisonous substances
    c. firearms
    d. gas inhalation

**True or False?** In the blank following each item, write T (for true) or F (for false). In the space below each item, if the statement is false, rewrite it to make it true.

1. Puberty begins with a sharp increase in the production of male and female hormones. _____

2. Among normal boys and girls, the time of onset of puberty varies by about 4 years. _____

3. Girls normally enter puberty about 2 or 3 years earlier than boys. _____

4. The age at which youngsters reach adult height and sexual maturity is genetically determined. _____

5. The adolescent growth spurt begins earlier in boys than in girls. _____

6. The principal sign of sexual maturity in boys is production of sperm. _____

7. Girls' age of first menstruation tends to be similar to their mothers'. _____

8. The first menstruation means that a girl can become pregnant. _____

9. Most young teenagers are more concerned about their looks than any other aspect of themselves. _____

10. Early-maturing boys tend to gain self-esteem. _____

11. Adolescents from poor families are 3 times as likely as others to be in fair or poor health. _____

12. Anorexia nervosa is the most common eating disorder in the United States. _____

13. Antidepressant drugs can be used in treating anorexia and bulimia. _____

14. Poverty is linked with drug abuse. _____

15. AIDS is caused by a bacterial infection. _____

16. Girls are more likely to commit suicide than boys. _____

17. Telephone hotlines are effective in preventing suicide. _____

# ANSWER KEY FOR CHAPTER 15

## CHAPTER 15 REVIEW

### Important Terms for Section I
1. adulthood
2. reproduce

### Important Terms for Section II
1. secular
2. height, weight
3. primary, secondary
4. secondary, primary
5. ejaculation
6. menstruation
7. testes, ovaries

### Important Terms for Section III
1. anorexia
2. bulimia
3. abuse
4. dependence
5. addictive
6. venereal

## CHAPTER 15 QUIZ

### Matching--Health Issues
1. k
2. f
3. b
4. c
5. g
6. d
7. l
8. e
9. h
10. a
11. j
12. i

### Multiple-Choice
1. b
2. b
3. b
4. a
5. d
6. b
7. b
8. d
9. b
10. d
11. b
12. d
13. a
14. c
15. d
16. b
17. a
18. c
19. c
20. c

### True or False?
1. T
2. F-Among normal boys and girls, the time of onset of puberty varies by about 7 years.
3. T
4. F-The age at which youngsters reach adult height and sexual maturity has been dropping in industrialized countries, apparently as a result of higher living standards.
5. F-The adolescent growth spurt begins earlier in girls.
6. T
7. T
8. F-Early menstrual periods usually do not include ovulation; many girls cannot conceive for 12 to 18 months after their first menstruation.
9. T
10. T
11. T
12. F-Obesity is the most common eating disorder in the United States.
13. T
14. F-Poverty is linked with drug abuse only if the deprivation is extreme.
15. F-AIDS is caused by a viral infection.
16. F-Boys are more likely to commit suicide.
17. F-The effectiveness of suicide prevention hotlines is minimal.

# CHAPTER 16
# COGNITIVE DEVELOPMENT IN ADOLESCENCE

## OVERVIEW

Chapter 16 examines progress in adolescents' cognitive development. In this chapter, the authors:

❑ Describe the dramatic changes in cognitive functioning that accompany the achievement of Piaget's stage of formal operations

❑ Examine what Elkind identified as immature aspects of adolescent thought

❑ Assess Kohlberg's theory of moral reasoning

❑ Discuss stresses connected with the transition to secondary school

❑ Examine influences on achievement in high school

❑ Outline stages in, and influences on, vocational planning

## GUIDEPOSTS FOR STUDY

16.1 How do adolescents' thinking and use of language differ from younger children's?

16.2 On what basis do adolescents make moral judgments?

16.3 What influences affect success in secondary school and why do some students drop out?

16.4 What factors affect educational and vocational planning and preparation?

## CHAPTER 16 REVIEW

### Section I Aspects of Cognitive Maturation

FRAMEWORK FOR SECTION I

A.      Piaget's Stage of Formal Operations
   1.   Hypothetical-Deductive Reasoning
   2.   Evaluating Piaget's Theory

B.      Language Development

C.      Elkind: Immature Characteristics of Adolescent Thought

### IMPORTANT TERMS FOR SECTION I

**Completion:** Fill in the blanks to complete the definitions of key terms for this section of Chapter 16.

1. **formal operations:** In Piaget's theory, the final stage of cognitive development, characterized by the ability to think _____.

2. **hypothetical-_____ reasoning:** Ability, believed by Piaget to accompany the stage of formal operations, to develop, consider, and test hypotheses.

3. _____: In Elkind's terminology, an observer who exists only in an adolescent's mind and is as concerned with the adolescent's thoughts and actions as the adolescent is.

4. **personal _____:** In Elkind's terminology, conviction that one is special, unique, and not subject to the rules that govern the rest of the world.

221

## LEARNING OBJECTIVES FOR SECTION I

After reading and reviewing this section of Chapter 16, you should be able to do the following.

1. Describe the capabilities characteristic of Piaget's stage of formal operations, particularly as illustrated by the pendulum problem.

2. Identify conditions that foster the achievement of cognitive maturity.

3. Give examples of practical applications of formal reasoning.

4. Cite some limitations identified by critics of Piaget's theory.

5. Describe six immature thought processes or behaviors typical of adolescents, according to Elkind, and summarize research on the validity of his concepts of the imaginary audience and personal fable.

**Section II Moral Reasoning: Kohlberg's Theory**

## FRAMEWORK FOR SECTION II

A.    Kohlberg's Levels and Stages
B.    Evaluating Kohlberg's Theory
    1.   Family Influences
    2.   Validity for Women and Girls

3. Cross-Cultural Validity

## IMPORTANT TERMS FOR SECTION II

**Completion:** Fill in the blanks to complete the definitions of key terms for this section of Chapter 16.

1. **preconventional morality:** First level of Kohlberg's theory of moral reasoning, in which control is external and rules are obeyed in order to gain rewards or avoid _____.

2. **conventional morality** or **morality of conventional role conformity:** Second level in Kohlberg's theory of moral reasoning, in which the standards of authority figures are _____.

3. **postconventional morality** or **morality of** _____ _____ _____: Third level in Kohlberg's theory of moral reasoning, in which people follow internally held moral principles of right and wrong, fairness, and justice, and can decide among conflicting moral standards.

## LEARNING OBJECTIVES FOR SECTION II

After reading and reviewing this section of Chapter 16, you should be able to do the following.

1. Identify and describe Kohlberg's three levels and original six stages of moral reasoning, and give a typical answer to a moral dilemma at each stage.

2. Explain why the ages attached to Kohlberg's stages are highly variable.

3. Assess criticisms of Kohlberg's theory.

4. Tell how interaction with parents can influence moral development.

5. Summarize research on gender differences in moral thinking.

6. Point out cross-cultural differences that challenge Kohlberg's system.

## Section III Educational and Vocational Issues
### FRAMEWORK FOR SECTION III

A.      Influences on School Achievement
     1.  Self-Efficacy Beliefs and Academic Motivation
     2.  Socioeconomic Status and the Family Environment
     3.  Parental Involvement and Parenting Styles
     4.  Ethnicity and Peer Influence
     5.  Quality of Schooling

B.      Dropping Out of High School

C.      Educational and Vocational Preparation
     1.  Influences on Student's Aspirations
     2.  Guiding Students Not Bound for College
     3.  Should High School Students Work Part Time?

### IMPORTANT TERMS FOR SECTION III

**Completion:** Fill in the blanks to complete the definitions of key terms for this section of Chapter 16.

    1.    **social** _____ : Family and community resources upon which a person can draw.

### LEARNING OBJECTIVES FOR SECTION III

After reading and reviewing this section of Chapter 16, you should be able to do the following.

  1.  Cite factors that may make the transition from elementary school to junior high more stressful than going from elementary school directly to high school, especially for girls.

  2.  List characteristics of a good high school, and explain why tracking may be harmful to low-achieving students.

3. Describe research on teaching and learning styles, based on the Sternberg Triarchic Abilities Test.

4. Tell how parenting styles, ethnic group attitudes, and socioeconomic status influence achievement in high school, including the importance of social capital.

5. Give arguments for and against part-time work for adolescents.

6. Outline three classic stages in vocational planning.

7. Discuss school dropout rates, factors that influence students to drop out, and dropout prevention.

8. Discuss influences on adolescents' vocational planning.

9. Explain the need for guidance of noncollege-bound youth in making the transition from school to work.

## CHAPTER 16 QUIZ

**Matching--Numbers:** Match each item in the left-hand column with the appropriate number from the right-hand column. (Note: Decimals have been rounded up or down to the nearest whole number.)

1. Approximate percentage of Americans 25 and older who are high school graduates _____

a.  83

2. Approximate age at which a person achieves the stage of formal operations, according to Piaget _____

b.  6

3. U.S. high school dropout rate (percent) in 1997 _____

c.  11

d.  4-5

4. Percentage of U.S. high school students who do not go on to college _____

5. Number of stages of moral development proposed by Kohlberg _____

e.  33

**Multiple-Choice:** Circle the choice that best completes or answers each item.

1. An adolescent who can think abstractly, imagine possibilities, and test hypotheses is in Piaget's stage of
    a.  concrete operations
    b.  scientific operations
    c.  logical operations
    d.  formal operations
2. A successful solution of the pendulum problem depends upon
    a.  careful observation
    b.  trial and error
    c.  inductive reasoning
    d.  varying one factor at a time
3. According to Piaget, cognitive maturity is the product of
    a.  neurological maturation
    b.  environmental stimulation
    c.  both a and b
    d.  neither a nor b
4. Piaget's definition of cognitive maturity has been criticized for failure to consider
    a.  nonscientific aspects of intelligence
    b.  women's perspective
    c.  cultural factors
    d.  socioeconomic factors

5. Although Frank, age 17, knows that drinking and driving is dangerous, he does it anyway. When his mother remonstrates, he tells her, "Get off my back, Mom--I'll be OK!" In Elkind's terminology, this is an example of
    a. argumentativeness
    b. the personal fable
    c. finding fault with authority figures
    d. apparent hypocrisy

6. According to Kohlberg, a person's level of moral reasoning is related to
    a. training by parents
    b. gender
    c. cognitive development
    d. cultural background

7. According to Kohlberg, people indicate their level of moral development by
    a. their answer to a moral dilemma
    b. the length of time they spend thinking about a moral dilemma
    c. the reasoning behind their answer to a moral dilemma
    d. the kinds of moral dilemmas they consider

8. In Kohlberg's third stage, maintaining mutual relations, children obey rules because they want to
    a. avoid punishment
    b. be rewarded
    c. do their duty
    d. please and help others

9. Most adolescents are at which of Kohlberg's levels of moral development?
    a. preconventional
    b. conventional
    c. postconventional
    d. unconventional

10. All but which of the following have contributed to doubts about Kohlberg's theory?
    a. Research has failed to confirm his proposed sequence of stages.
    b. In some studies, men scored higher than women.
    c. People in nonwestern cultures score lower than westerners.
    d. The link between hypothetical and actual behavior is not clear.

11. Parents can best foster adolescents' moral development by
    a. letting them work out ethical dilemmas on their own
    b. asking clarifying questions
    c. giving advice
    d. lecturing

12. Parents whose children do well in high school tend to be those who
    a. encourage children to look at both sides of an issue
    b. teach children not to argue with adults
    c. "ground" children who get low grades
    d. leave it up to children to do their homework

13. High school students with authoritative parents tend to be higher achievers and better adjusted, regardless of all but which of the following?
    a. gender
    b. family structure
    c. social class
    d. ethnicity

14. A longitudinal study in St. Paul found that high school seniors who work more than 20 hours a week tend to
    a. get lower grades than other students
    b. drink more than other students
    c. feel depressed and overburdened
    d. have behavior problems at school

15. Which of the following statements about the relationship between socioeconomic status and achievement in high school is true?
    a. Parents' educational and occupational levels are determining factors in student achievement.
    b. Socioeconomic status is only weakly related to student achievement.
    c. Socioeconomic status indirectly affects student achievement through its influence on family and school atmosphere.
    d. There is no significant relationship between socioeconomic status and student achievement.

16. Which of the following is most likely to drop out of high school?
    a. Latino
    b. African American
    c. non-Latino white
    d. All of the above are equally likely to drop out.

17. <u>All but which</u> of the following have been found to affect the risk of dropping out of high school?
    a. active engagement
    b. social capital
    c. family structure
    d. temperament

18. Which of the following statements about parental influence on educational aspirations is true?
    a. Children of well-to-do parents have the highest aspirations.
    b. Children's aspirations for themselves tend to be quite different from their parents' aspirations for them.
    c. Parental encouragement predicts children's high aspirations better than social class does.
    d. none of the above; no connection between parental influence and children's educational aspirations has been found

**True or False?** In the blank following each item, write T (for true) or F (for false). In the space below each item, if the statement is false, rewrite it to make it true.

1. According to the Piagetian perspective, adolescents' idealism is a sign of cognitive immaturity. _____

2. Almost all adults reach cognitive maturity. _____

3. The imaginary audience and the personal fable seem to be universal features of adolescent cognitive development. _____

4. Kohlberg believed that morality results from internalizing the standards of parents and teachers. _____

5. A person at Kohlberg's postconventional level of morality can choose between two socially accepted moral standards. _____

6. A high level of cognitive development produces an equally high level of moral development. _____

7. Gilligan's claim that Kohlberg's theory is oriented toward male values has been upheld by the preponderance of research. _____

8. The transition to high school tends to be more stressful for youngsters who go to junior high school than for those who enter high school directly after 8 years of elementary school. _____

9. Among 25- to 29-year-olds, the percentages of black and white high school graduates are statistically equal. _____

10. Low-ability students do better when placed in classes with students of equal ability. _____

11. Teenagers who describe their parents as authoritarian or permissive tend to attribute poor grades to forces beyond their control. _____

12. Teenagers who work after school tend to get lower grades than teenagers who do not work after school. _____

13. Dropouts are more likely than high school graduates to become involved with drugs. _____

14. The high school dropout rate in the United States is increasing. _____

15. Students in fairly affluent single-parent or remarried households are more likely to drop out of high school than students living with both parents. _____

16. About one- third of U.S. high school graduates do not go to college. _____

## ANSWER KEY FOR CHAPTER 16

**CHAPTER 16 REVIEW**

**Important Terms for Section I**

1. abstractly
2. deductive
3. imaginary audience
4. fable

**Important Terms for Section II**

1. punishment
2. internalized
3. autonomous moral principles

**Important Terms for Section III**

1. capital

## CHAPTER 16 QUIZ

**Matching**

1. a
2. c
3. d
4. e
5. b

**Multiple-Choice**

1. d
2. d
3. c
4. a
5. b
6. c
7. c
8. d
9. b
10. a
11. b
12. a
13. d
14. b
15. c
16. a
17. d
18. c

**True or False?**

1. F-According to the Piagetian perspective, adolescents' idealism is a sign of attainment of cognitive maturity, the capacity for abstract thought.
2. F-Up to one-half of American adults apparently never reach cognitive maturity, as measured by formal operations tasks.
3. F-The imaginary audience and personal fable do <u>not</u> seem to be universal features of adolescent cognitive development.
4. F-Kohlberg believed that morality is the result of reasoned judgments that people work out on their own.
5. T
6. F-Factors other than cognition affect moral reasoning; advanced cognitive development is necessary for advanced moral development but does not guarantee it.
7. F-The weight of the evidence does not support a claim of male bias in Kohlberg's theory.
8. T
9. T
10. F-Placing low-ability students in classes with other low-ability students often results in lack of stimulation, poorer teaching, loss of interest in studies, and solidification of problem behaviors.
11. T
12. F-Findings on effects of after-school work on grades are mixed.
13. T
14. F-The high school dropout rate has declined since 1980.
15. T
16. T

# PSYCHOSOCIAL DEVELOPMENT IN ADOLESCENCE

## OVERVIEW

Chapter 17 focuses on the profound and sometimes disquieting personality developments that accompany the physical and cognitive changes of adolescence. In this chapter, the authors:

❑ Present theory and research on adolescent boys' and girls' search for identity

❑ Examine sexual attitudes and practices among adolescents

❑ Explore causes, consequences, prevention, and treatment of teenage pregnancy

❑ Describe teenagers' relationships with parents, siblings, and peers

❑ Discuss parental and peer influences on antisocial behavior and juvenile delinquency, and report on the success of early prevention programs for high-risk youth

❑ Compare adolescents' attitudes and self-image in 10 cultures throughout the world

## GUIDEPOSTS FOR STUDY

17.1  How do adolescents form an identity?

17.2  What determines sexual orientation?

17.3  What sexual practices are common among adolescents and what leads some to engage in risky sexual behavior?

17.4  How common is teenage pregnancy, and what are its usual outcomes?

17.5  How typical is "adolescent rebellion"?

17.6  How do adolescents relate to parents, siblings, and peers?

17.7  What are the root causes of antisocial behavior and juvenile delinquency and what can be done to reduce these and other risks of adolescence?

17.8  How does adolescence vary across cultures and what are some common psychosocial features?

## CHAPTER 17 REVIEW

**Section I The Search for Identity**

FRAMEWORK FOR SECTION I

A.      Erikson: Identity Versus Identity Confusion

B.      Marcia:Identity Status: Crisis and Commitment

C.      Gender Differences in Identity Formation

D.      Ethnic Factors in Identity Formation

E.      Elkind: The Patchwork Self

## IMPORTANT TERMS FOR SECTION I

**Completion:** Fill in the blanks to complete the definitions of key terms for this section of Chapter 17.

1. **identity versus identity _____:** In Erikson's theory, the fifth crisis of psychosocial development, in which an adolescent seeks to develop a coherent sense of self, including the role she or he is to play in society. Also called <u>identity versus role</u> _____.

2. **identity statuses:** In Marcia's terminology, states of ego development which depend on the presence or absence of _____ and _____.

3. **crisis:** In Marcia's terminology, period of _____ decision making related to identity formation.

4. **commitment:** In Marcia's terminology, personal investment in an occupation or system of

   _____.

5. **identity _____:** Identity status, described by Marcia, which is characterized by commitment to choices made following a crisis, a period spent in exploring alternatives.

6. **_____:** Identity status, described by Marcia, in which a person who has not spent time considering alternatives (that is, has not been in crisis) is committed to other people's plans for his or her life.

7. **_____:** Identity status, described by Marcia, in which a person is currently considering alternatives (in crisis) and seems headed for commitment.

8. **Identity _____:** Identity status, described by Marcia, which is characterized by absence of commitment and lack of serious consideration of alternatives.


## LEARNING OBJECTIVES FOR SECTION I

After reading and reviewing this section of Chapter 17, you should be able to do the following.

1. Discuss how identity formation occurs in adolescence, according to Erikson, and name the three main issues involved in the identity crisis.

2. Name the two elements that determine identity status, according to Erikson and James Marcia, and describe four categories of identity status identified by Marcia.

3. Compare Erikson's, Marcia's, and Gilligan's views on gender differences in identity formation, and summarize research findings on how gender affects self-esteem.

4. Explain how ethnicity can complicate identity formation for young people in minority groups.

**Section II Sexuality**

## FRAMEWORK FOR SECTION II

A.  Sexual Orientation

B.  Sexual Behavior
   1.  The Sexual Evolution
   2.  Homosexual Identity and Behavior

C.  Sexual Risk Taking
   1.  Early Sexual Activity
   2.  Use of Contraceptives
   3.  Where Do Teenagers Get Information about Sex

D.  Teenage Pregnancy and Childbearing

## LEARNING OBJECTIVES FOR SECTION II

After reading and reviewing this section of Chapter 17, you should be able to do the following.

1. Name three difficulties of studying adolescents' sexuality.

2. Discuss the reasons for, and effects of, the evolution in sexual behavior and attitudes among adolescents in recent years.

3. Identify three patterns of risky sexual behavior, and three major risks that accompany it.

4. Discuss reasons for early sexual activity and factors that influence its likelihood.

5. Identify trends in contraceptive use and characteristics of adolescents who do not use reliable protection when engaging in sexual behavior.

6. Discuss the connection between sexual knowledge and rates of sexual activity, and compare the effectiveness of knowledge gained from parents or other adults, from formal instruction, and from the media.

7. Give at least two reasons for the high teenage pregnancy rates in the United States as compared with most Western European industrialized countries, discuss implications for public policy, and describe a promising pregnancy prevention program.

8. Identify characteristics of teenagers who are likely to become pregnant and of the fathers of babies born to teenage mothers.

9. Describe trends in teenage pregnancy and birth rates among married and unwed girls.

10. Identify the practical and emotional needs of expectant teenagers, and ways of helping them adjust to parenthood.

11. Cite problems that contribute to poor outcomes of teenage pregnancy for mothers and children.

12. Discuss benefits and drawbacks of a teenage mother's living with her own mother.

**Section III Relationships with Family, Peers, and Adult Society**

FRAMEWORK FOR SECTION III

A.  Is Adolescent Rebellion a Myth?

B.  How Adolescents Spend Their Time – and with Whom?

B.  Adolescents and Parents
   1. Family Conflict
   2. Parenting Styles
   3. Economic Stress
   4. Sibling Relationships

C.  Adolescents and Siblings

D.  Peers and Friends
   1. Popularity
   2. Friendships

D.  Antisocial Behavior and Juvenile Delinquency
   1. Becoming a Delinquent: How Parental and Peer Influences Interact
   2. Long-Term Prospects
   3. Preventing and Treating Delinquency

# IMPORTANT TERM FOR SECTION III

**Completion:** Fill in the blank to complete the definition of the key term for this section of Chapter 17.

1. **adolescent rebellion:** Pattern of emotional turmoil, characteristic of a minority of adolescents, which may involve conflict with family, alienation from adult society, and hostility toward adults'

   _____.

# LEARNING OBJECTIVES FOR SECTION III

After reading and reviewing this section of Chapter 17, you should be able to do the following.

1. Evaluate the validity of the concept of adolescent rebellion, and explain the danger of assuming that adolescent turmoil is normal and necessary.

2. Describe cross-cultural research on the continuity of personality types from childhood through adolescence.

3. Tell how teenagers typically allocate their time, particularly the changes in time spent with family and peers; and point out cultural differences.

4. Describe the typical nature and extent of adolescent conflict with parents and its course from early to late adolescence, and point out ethnic variations.

5. Discuss the relationship between family atmosphere, parenting styles, and family conflict, and identify the kind of parenting that seems to best meet adolescents' needs.

6. Assess effects of parents' employment on adolescents.

7. Assess the effects of family structure and economic stress on adolescents' well-being.

8. Describe changes in sibling relationships during adolescence and cite factors that may influence the quality of these relationships.

9. Identify five peer status groups, and tell which groups have the greatest adjustment problems.

10. Tell how friendship in adolescence differs from friendship during childhood, and cite factors affecting its quality.

11. Tell how parental and peer influences interact, from early childhood on, to promote antisocial or delinquent behavior.

12. Cite factors affecting the likelihood that antisocial teenagers will become chronic delinquents or hard-core criminals.

13. Discuss the impact of early childhood intervention in preventing delinquency.

## Section IV Is There a "Universal Adolescent"?

## LEARNING OBJECTIVE FOR SECTION IV

After reading and reviewing this section of Chapter 17, you should be able to do the following.

1. Discuss findings of cross-cultural studies of adolescents' attitudes and self-image.

# CHAPTER 17 QUIZ

**Matching--Who's Who:** Match each name in the left-hand column with the appropriate description in the right-hand column. (Note: Here, a description may be used to identify more than one name.)

1. David Elkind _____
2. Margaret Mead _____
3. Sigmund Freud _____
4. Lawrence Kohlberg _____
5. Erik Erikson _____
6. James E. Marcia _____
7. Carol Gilligan _____
8. Daniel Offer _____

a. categorized identity statuses
b. found cross-cultural similarities in adolescent self-image
c. held that parent-child friction comes from the adolescent's need for independence
d. sense of identity constructed by substituting other people's attitudes, beliefs, and commitment for one's own
e. held that the chief task of adolescence is to resolve the identity crisis
f. studied adolescence in nonwestern cultures
g. held that females achieve identity through relationships
h. delinquent and predelinquent teenagers tend to be stuck in stage 2 of this moral reasoning

**Multiple-Choice:** Circle the choice that best completes or answers each item.

1. According to Erikson, a major aspect of the adolescent's search for identity is the
   a. first sexual relationship
   b. changing relationship with parents
   c. choice of occupation
   d. choice of a peer group

2. The "virtue" that arises from Erikson's identity crisis is
   a. fidelity
   b. industry
   c. self-esteem
   d. independence

3. Erin has never experienced an identity crisis. She and her father have always been close. When he advised her to get an MBA and go into business, she took his advice. After getting her degree, she accepted a position with a large bank and made a down payment on a house. When she sees her friends agonizing over their career choices, Erin smiles with a trace of superiority. James Marcia would place Erin in the category of
   a. identity achievement
   b. foreclosure
   c. identity confusion
   d. moratorium

4. According to Gilligan, women achieve identity primarily through
   a. cooperation
   b. competition
   c. crisis
   d. careers

5. Findings on sexual practices may be inaccurate because
   a. volunteers tend to be less sexually active than the population as a whole
   b. sexual attitudes are constantly changing
   c. subjects may not be truthful, and self-reports cannot be corroborated
   d. all of the above

6. The average girl has her first sexual experience at age
   a. 11
   b. 13
   c. 15
   d. 17

7. What proportion of U.S. adolescents use birth control during their first sexual experience?
   a. one-fourth
   b. one-third
   c. one-half
   d. two-thirds

8. The pregnancy rate in the United States for girls age 15 to 19 is about
    a. 5 percent
    b. 10 percent
    c. 25 percent
    d. 40 percent

9. All but which of the following are major factors in a teenage girl's likelihood of becoming pregnant?
    a. age of sexual initiation
    b. sexual knowledge
    c. sexual desire
    d. accessibility of family planning services

10. According to one study, all but which of the following are the most important considerations cited by U.S. teenagers as influencing their use of a birth control clinic?
    a. location
    b. cost
    c. service
    d. confidentiality

11. Which of the following is not a likely consequence of teenage pregnancy today?
    a. birth complications
    b. end or postponement of schooling
    c. low-birthweight baby
    d. quick adoption

12. Which of the following adolescents is likely to maintain more intimate family relationships and less intense peer relationships?
    a. white
    b. black
    c. both a and b
    d. neither a nor b

13. The psychologist who described adolescence as a time of "storm and stress" was
    a. G. Stanley Hall
    b. Sigmund Freud
    c. Anna Freud
    d. Erik Erikson

14. Margaret Mead's research on stress in adolescence highlights the importance of
    a. heredity
    b. culture
    c. sexuality
    d. maturation

15. The percentage of families in which serious conflict between adolescents and parents occurs is approximately
    a. 5 to 10
    b. 15 to 25
    c. 35 to 40
    d. 50 to 60

16. Which of the following usually is not an issue in arguments between adolescents and their parents?
    a. values
    b. schoolwork
    c. chores
    d. friends

17. Discord between adolescents and parents generally
    a. increases steadily during the teenage years
    b. increases during early adolescence, then decreases steadily during middle and late adolescence
    c. increases during early adolescence, then stabilizes during middle adolescence and decreases in late adolescence
    d. does not follow any particular pattern

18. Adolescents whose mothers are employed tend to
    a. show poorer social adjustment than other adolescents
    b. have more conflict with their families
    c. be more subject to peer pressure
    d. have lower self-esteem

19. On the basis of their sociometric classifications, which of the following adolescents is likely to do well in school?
    a. rejected youngster
    b. neglected youngster
    c. controversial youngster
    d. none of the above

20. Adolescents tend to choose friends who are
    a. physically attractive
    b. outgoing
    c. athletic
    d. like themselves

21. All but which of the following are likely predictors of chronic delinquency?
    a. falling in with "the wrong crowd"
    b. low-income neighborhood
    c. harsh or inconsistent parenting during early childhood
    d. poor communication with mother during early adolescence

**True or False?** In the blank following each item, write T (for true) or F (for false). In the space below each item, if the statement is false, rewrite it to make it true.

1. According to Erikson, women cannot achieve mature intimacy until they have achieved identity. _____

2. According to Marcia, it may be just as healthy for women to achieve identity with or without going through a crisis. _____

3. Studies suggest that high school girls tend to have higher self-esteem than high school boys. _____

4. Sexual activity among teenagers has steadily increased since the 1970s. _____

5. Early, frequent sexual activity is related to antisocial behavior. _____

6. Adolescent girls who feel ashamed of engaging in premarital sex are more likely than other girls to use effective contraception. _____

7. School sex education programs tend to lead to more sexual activity. _____

8. Most fathers of babies born to teenage mothers are teenagers themselves. _____

9. Teenage pregnancy and birth rates are rising. _____

10. Most teenage mothers and their babies do better when they live with the mother's mother. _____

11. According to self-reports in a Chicago area study, adolescents spend about 14 percent of waking hours with their families. _____

12. Research confirms Freud's belief in the inevitability of adolescent rebellion. _____

13. European American and Asian American adolescents are more likely to have conflicts with their fathers than with their mothers. _____

14. Authoritarian parenting is the most effective style with adolescents because it gives them strict limits. _____

15. Adolescents who are home alone after school are vulnerable to peer pressure for antisocial behavior. _____

16. Teenage siblings who are close in age tend to get along better than those who are spaced farther apart. _____

17. Adolescent friendships tend to be more intense than childhood or adult friendships. _____

18. Juvenile delinquents tend to commit crimes when they become adults. _____

19. Early childhood intervention programs have been effective in preventing juvenile delinquency. _____

20. In Daniel Offer's cross-cultural research on adolescents' self-image, most adolescents had negative feelings toward their parents. _____

# ANSWER KEY FOR CHAPTER 17

## CHAPTER 17 REVIEW

### Important Terms for Section I
1. confusion, confusion
2. crisis, commitment
3. conscious
4. beliefs
5. achievement
6. foreclosure
7. moratorium
8. diffusion

### Important Term for Section III
1. values

## CHAPTER 17 QUIZ

### Matching--Who's Who
1. d
2. f
3. c
4. h
5. e
6. a
7. g
8. b

### Multiple-Choice
1. c
2. a
3. b
4. a
5. c
6. d
7. d
8. b
9. c
10. d
11. b
12. a
13. b
14. b
15. a
16. c
17. c
18. c
19. d
20. a
21. a

### True or False?
1. F-According to Erikson, men cannot achieve mature intimacy until they have achieved identity, but women achieve identity through intimacy.
2. T
3. F-Studies suggests that high school boys' self-esteem exceeds that of girls, whereas girls' self-esteem drops during adolescence.
4. F-Sexual activity among teenagers has declined during the 1990s, after rising between the 1970s and 1990.
5. T
6. F-Adolescent girls who feel ashamed about premarital sex are less likely than other girls to use effective contraception.
7. F-School sex education programs do not lead to more sexual activity.
8. F-Most fathers of babies born to teenage mothers are beyond their teens.
9. F-Teenage pregnancy and birth rates have declined during the 1990s.
10. F-Although findings are mixed, advantages of living with the infant's grandmother seem to lessen or reverse when the arrangement is long-term.
11. T
12. F-Research suggests that rebellion is not a necessary hallmark of adolescence.
13. F-European American and Asian American adolescents are more likely to have conflicts with their mothers than with their fathers.
14. F-Authoritative parenting is the most effective style with adolescents; it exercises appropriate control of behavior while respecting the adolescent's opinions and sense of self.
15. F-Lack of direct supervision does not, in itself, create vulnerability, so long as parents consistently monitor their child's whereabouts and activities.
16. F-Teenage siblings who are farther apart in years tend to get along better than those who are closer in age.
17. T
18. F-Except for "hard-core" offenders, most delinquent teenagers do not grow up to be criminals.
19. T
20. F – In Offer's research, 9 out of 10 adolescents in 10 countries had positive feelings toward their parents.

20. F – In Offer's research, 9 out of 10 adolescents in 10 countries had positive feelings toward their parents.